Un

Unleashing
<u>*Your Passion*</u>

And Stepping Into Your Greatness

A series of uplifting books presented by Living a Fulfilled Life
Series 2

Inspiring and educating the world
while helping and supporting people everywhere

Unleashing Your Passion
Copyright © 2017 by J. Drew Bycoskie. All rights reserved

While the author has made every effort to provide accurate information relating to web-sites and Internet addresses at the time of publication, the author does not assume any responsibility for errors or for changes that occur after publication.
Second Edition: January 2017
This is a modification rewrite of the original Pulling in Your Passion from 2014 as copyrighted by J. Drew Bycoskie

Library of Congress Cataloging-In Publication Data
J. Drew Bycoskie
Unleashing Your Passion
ISBN:

Acknowledgments:

Thank you to the many individuals that participated and/or contributed in creating this book. It is humbly dedicated to the wonderful and brave people that are afflicted with ALS, Lou Gehrig's disease. You are a great inspiration to us all.

A special thanks to my sister Pam and my fiance Tina for their ongoing support and guidance.

To my three beautiful daughters, Chloe, Bergen and Elly, I love you with all my heart. In loving memory of my mother and father, Catherine Cecilia Bycoskie and John Bycoskie.

CONTENTS

Visit us on the web at **www.livingafulfilledlife.net**

*"There is not a more perfect time than the present
to embark upon the pursuit of your passion.
Seize this opportunity to define your future by
Unleashing Your Passion."*

~ *J. Drew Bycoskie*

INTRODUCTION

To me, having a passion affords me the bountiful opportunity to be the person that I truly desire to be. Pursuing my passion gives me fulfillment. It makes me whole and allows me to live a unique life experience. It's an extraordinary journey to find your passion - living every day in a paradise where you have the freedom to be a unique and fulfilled person.

Is your life making you happy? Do your friends make you happy? If you left the Earth tomorrow, would you depart feeling like your life had meaning and purpose? How will you be remembered?

If the answers are all positive, then congratulations, you have found purpose and passion in your life. If you hesitated on any of the questions, I'd be glad to help you embark on the expedition to begin searching for the positives in your life. Even though there was a voice inside me that needed to be heard, it took a near-death experience to get me to listen. I needed to begin searching for my own passion. I battled my uncontrolled emotions and faced my deepest fears to conquer the forces that had buried my passion within me. After much struggle, I learned I am the eye of the tiger.

Passion is within you and it's what gives your life purpose and meaning. Only you can unleash it. It's hard and yet it's so simple. You've heard the platitudes and cliches until they've become nothing more than gibberish, maybe something you read on a greeting card or a poster somewhere. But have you ever thought about what your life really needs? We'll dust off some of the sage cliches of the masters and also explore the advice offered by experts. I'll even share some of my own experiences with you. I'll help you find your passion.

Everyone deserves to live a fulfilled life full of meaning and purpose. OK, here comes a cliche. *You need to stop and smell the flowers.* While you're at it, take a look at the colors of your life to see if they're still vibrant.

I'm going to encourage you to rattle your cage. Unleash Your Passion. I dare you. I promise you that life on the other side will be a kaleidescope of color and, without a doubt, more passionate.

When someone asks you the question, *Are you happy?* You'll answer without hesitation, *Yes, I'm happy.*

Finding you passion and purpose is like finding your personal road map to a fulfilled life. A Passion Map is a unique life map that provides meaning, direction and purpose. When you identify your purpose to unleash your passion, you are truly living a singularly unique life experience.

Contrary to the idea that doing what you love makes work effortless, a passion puts you to work. Obviously, our time on earth is a nanosecond in relation to the 4.5 billion years our planet has been in existence. We should, therefore, live our nanosecond to the fullest. The down-to-Earth, Academy Award winning actor, Jimmy Stewart, believed our lives are identified by a *begin date* and an *end date* with a definitive **dash** mark separating the two. The dash mark or hyphen represents the actual life of the individual. What will you do with your *dash*? When you look back on your life, will you be happy with the *dash* mark that you created?

Each of us only gets one *dash* - no one gets two. Young people live in the future, old people live in the past, and wise people live in the present.

"You may delay, but time will not."
~Benjamin Franklin

If you knew your time was short, would you do things differently? If you could turn back the clock to yesterday, would you have approached the day in a more positive and upbeat fashion? Are you questioning both the past and some of the short-cuts you may have taken, consciously or subconsciously? Are you unprepared for tomorrow and operating with a state of mind clouded with uncertainty?

The Dalai Lama wisely asks, "What are you going to do with your life that you now have?" Are you going to do something that provides meaning, purpose and fulfillment? Living a life full of purpose and meaning will not only make you more optimistic, you will also be more compassionate and fulfilled - exuding all the qualities of someone who has found happiness. It is your obligation to not only identify your passion and purpose, but to exercise that passion every day. If you are able to harness your passion, you will not only fulfill your own life prophecy, you will have a positive impact on those around you.

At times, we all wonder ponder our existence. What is our higher calling and how can we explore our eternal legacy to provide meaning and purpose in our lives? How can we identify and incorporate passions and dreams into our daily lives in order to reach our highest potential? We are all pinched with the demands of career, relationships, school and parenting, which can stifle our ability to openly explore life's inner calling, purpose and passion.

You, like many people, often procrastinate thereby continuously delaying your individual prophecy. That allows your mind to cultivate negative behavior, self-defeating thoughts and excuses, which in turn, hinders your exploration of purpose.

Make a conscious decision to grow stronger mentally, physically and spiritually? Perhaps you are comfortable with who you are today and not necessarily concerned with reaching for a fulfilled tomorrow. Yet, deep down inside, you occasionally feel a void in life and the direction you've chosen. The realization that your current journey in life needs to be refocused due to many circumstances that have left us unfulfilled can be alarming.

Our subconscious has an uncanny way of reminding us that we are not living up to our potential. As Les Brown, a motivational speaker and life coach so accurately conveys, "If you want to keep getting what you're getting, keep doing what you're doing." Very simply, if you have chosen to identify and embark upon your passion journey, then you need to change both your thoughts and actions today.

"If you want to keep getting what you're getting,
keep doing what you're doing."

~ Les Brown

The intent and focus of this book is to explore the importance of unleashing your passions, which ultimately provides direction, guidance and hope. A life without passion and conviction can potentially manifest itself into emptiness, sorrow and a lackluster disposition that may cloud the very essence of who you are. As you bravely venture into this book, it is my hope and expectation that you will learn why you have not taken the initiative in exploring your life's purpose or passion.

What obstacles or hurdles prevent you from identifying and pursuing life's purpose and meaning? Anger, limiting beliefs, fear of success, procrastination and bad attitudes are just a few of the obstacles that often prevent you from living a life of passion and purpose. These destructive impediments will be scrutinized in this book. Once these barriers have been identified, I have put together a plan of action to eliminate these barriers and self-defeating habits.

Next, you will begin to identify your passion and purpose. This strategy is an accumulation of my thoughts and experiences combined with the ideas and suggestions of other notable authors and speakers. The objective of this strategy is to provide direction to help you identify your passion. By incorporating both my thoughts with the sage advice of notable passion enthusiasts, I am able to help individuals eliminate their self-defeating barriers and embark on the journey of finding purpose and passion. I am very grateful for the generous contributions that have been made to pen this book.

This book continues with the wonderful and brave stories of five individuals who have been blessed to be living their life with passion and purpose. Their remarkable stories and true sacrifices will provide inspiration, direction and guidance to begin the process of identifying and pursuing the true passion and purpose in your life.

"The consequences of today are determined by the actions of the past. To change your future, alter your decisions today."
~Unknown

About The Author: Drew Bycoskie

Like so many of us, I ponder the true meaning of life and our higher calling or purpose in life. Reaching middle-age and reassessing my life at every turn, my journey of self-discovery continues. I embark on this journey with vigor and enthusiasm, yet I am confronted with frustration more times than I want to admit. As we start the aging process and move beyond middle age, I believe that we all come to the conclusion that we have finite time on this Earth.

I was born and raised in Malvern, Pa., in an upper-middle class suburban neighborhood near Philadelphia. My father was a high school chemistry teacher and my mother worked as an X-ray technician at the local hospital. Both taught me the values of hard work, dedication and commitment.

After graduating from Pennsylvania State University with a bachelor's degree in 1986 and a short one-year football coaching stint at Widener University, I began my graduate studies at the Widener University School of Management in 1988. Shortly thereafter, I started working for corporate America. For the past 25 years, I embraced working with two Fortune 100 companies in strategic leadership positions relating to sales execution, marketing, product development and product roll-out. I was located in both Los Angeles and the Greater Philadelphia area, which exposed me to people of many cultures and varying mindsets. Despite my success in the corporate world, the stifling bureaucracy left me feeling unsatisfied, frustrated and cynical.

Like so many career driven individuals, I was comfortable and reliant on the steady pay, the 401K, as well as the pension and benefits that came with my job. Through my professional experience and the erudite pursuit to earn an executive MBA from the Widener School of Management, I developed a think-outside-the-box attitude. I became increasingly interested in entrepreneurial pursuits. A series of events led me to take a leap of faith to orchestrate and manage two businesses in tax consulting and real estate development. Even though both businesses provided the essential food, shelter and vacation money for my growing family during the boom days of the past millennium, I still felt a lack of fulfillment.

Reflecting on my 25-year career and the diverse background that I have in sales and marketing, the recurring theme of my personal strengths and natural calling had clearly emerged. My ability to connect with individuals both professionally and socially has always been my strongest attribute. This ability and natural gift always helps me to stand out among my peers. Through my professional associations with top executives, managers, sales personnel and entry level employees, I was able to distinguish myself because of my unique ability to communicate and inspire others. Time management, organizational paper shuffling, conforming to corporate culture, and a rigid company structure were not exactly my strengths. Over the years, I came to the realize that I had the keen ability to motivate, direct and consult people on a wide array of topics ranging from business, human development and personal growth.

More importantly, I had a sincere passion and desire to help people elevate their calling and pursue their life goals. Even though I had never pursued my passion on a full time basis, my natural calling began to evolve as I began interviewing and talking to people who had successfully identified then pursued their passions. The exhilaration that I felt talking with people who had identified their life purpose became a true life mission for me. I wanted to learn from them and incorporate that learning into my daily life.

I wanted to immerse myself in the energy and enthusiasm of these passionate people who understood their own purpose. What was different about their mental and spiritual mindset in relation to mine? Was there a spiritual connection between individuals that had identified and pursued their passions that was absent in those that did not? All these questions had bubbled to the surface to ignite my curiosity and inner passion. It didn't take me long to realize what my passion in life is, and then I knew exactly what I am going to be doing for a very long time.

My purpose in life had evolved into helping others identify and implement creative ways to understand and utilize their own purpose in life through their own passions. As a coach, parent, working professional and author, I wanted to take my knowledge and passion to the next level by guiding others to identify their own purpose and passion. When someone finds his or her true passion and purpose, a light goes on deep inside as a heart begins to glow. That fire of positive energy resonates in the world around them, in career, family, social groups, and more. It is a polar shift from living an uninspired life to living an inspired life.

To help inspire others to pursue their passion in life, I have openly shared both my life experiences to convey how I was able to tap into my higher calling along with sharing the courageous journeys of others to provide you with the direction and motivation to begin on your path to happiness and fulfillment. The inspiration and impetus for writing this book was through a second heart attack I suffered in 2013.

Without knowing it, I was suffering from a life-threatening medical condition called Myocarditis, which is a viral infection that attacks the middle layer of the heart wall. As I laid in the emergency room hooked up to EKG machines and a myriad of monitors, I had an epiphany about my life and how disappointed I was that I had not reached my potential in many ways. My *dash* mark in life was not complete and definitely not up to the standards that I would have liked. I was obviously concerned and disappointed with my legacy as a human being, father and overall good person. As I laid helplessly in the hospital bed, alone and scared, I remember pondering if God was going to provide me yet another chance to pursue a more purposeful life.

I knew in my heart, no pun intended, that I had not reached my purpose in life. At times, I had taken shortcuts and not lived up to my potential. I was cheating life and definitely not defining my passion. Additionally, I was not utilizing my inherent blessings to help others. If God would allow me to recover, what would I do differently? How could I change to make my life and the lives of others more fulfilled and purposeful? At that moment, I made the concise and conscious decision that I was going to take my life back and accelerate the process of enhancing my *dash* mark. I promised myself to strengthen my own passion and purpose by helping others to identify theirs. There is no time like the present, so what was I waiting for? I wanted to exercise my free will and enhance my story by creating inspiration, direction and hope to others as well as to myself.

Passion and purpose are the natural fuels that help drive ordinary individuals to achieve extraordinary results. However, pursuit of your passion and purpose can be elusive. As we venture together in the pursuit of passion and purpose, I welcome the opportunity to help you take your life to the next level. I will help you to find clarity and meaning in your life. Since finding your passion can be an elusive pursuit, you must first understand exactly what the word in this context means.

CHAPTER 1

WHAT IS PASSION?

"Passion. It lies in all of us. Sleeping… waiting… and though unwanted, unbidden… it will stir… open its jaws and howl. It speaks to us… guides us. Passion rules us all. And we obey. What other choice do we have?"

– Joss Whedon

Passion is the energy that comes from bringing more of yourself into what you do. Simply put, it's being who you are and doing what comes naturally. When what you do is in alignment with what is in your soul and heart, you naturally get energy from doing it. It's like water flowing along its natural river bed. It gains energy from the path it is taking. Knowing your passion in life gives you something to build the rest of your life around, which ultimately will create a better life for you. Your passion can be anything that simultaneously challenges you, intrigues you and empowers you in an enthusiastic fashion. Contrary to the idea that doing what you love makes work effortless, a passion puts you to work. Your passion is the reason you wake up in the morning and the excitement of it can keep you up late at night.

To help better explain the emotion of living your passion, you must think of those moments where you challenged yourself and won. Perhaps you were a pianist in the high school orchestra and after long hours and months of arduous practice, the school concert represented the accolades of your hard work and dedication. The applause from the audience and recognition from peers and family was overwhelming. A euphoric feeling of bliss, jubilation and accomplishment was wrapped up as if a present to your self-esteem.

As a former athlete, blissful sports-related memories often echo in my mind. Encouragement and praise from family and the community that awarded me an athletic scholarship, accolades for personal and team achievements, camaraderie and forming lifelong bonds with teammates, were among the many advantages I have enjoyed. My experience with sports enhanced my spirit with positive energy to create a natural glow, a feeling of invincibility and an impenetrable mountain of self-worthiness. Playing on two national championship teams with Penn State football back in the 1980s provides a euphoric feeling that I carry with me to this day. The feeling of stepping onto a football field with 65,000 fans cheering and yelling your name is electrifying. I remember vividly the wonderful feeling and sense of accomplishment when I scored a touchdown or made a game winning tackle. To this day, I try to replicate those feelings of bliss by inspiring individuals and organizations to reach for and obtain their passions and goals. Once you identify your purpose and pursue your passion, you'll be able to live each day with an energized life experience that will maximize the *dash* in your life.

Case Study No. 1
Conversations with Gary Guller: World-Record Holder

I had the privilege to spend time with a remarkable gentleman named Gary Guller, who is the first one-armed person to ever climb Mt. Everest. A native of Britain, Gary has earned numerous accolades over the years as a mountaineer, motivational speaker, and true humanitarian.

In 2003, Gary guided the largest ever cross-disability group to reach the Mount Everest Base camp at 17,500 feet. Following that record-setting climb. Gary then went on to scale to the peak of Mt. Everest, which he reached on May 23, 2003.

Over his illustrious career, Gary has competed in the Marathon des Sables (world's toughest endurance stage race across the Sahara desert), trekked and climbed in the Nepal Himalayas, Europe, South America and produced a TV show highlighting his Team Everest quest.

Equally impressive, Gary has climbed to the peak of Mountain Cho Oyu in Tibet, China, which is the sixth highest peak in the world. He also scaled Mount Kilimanjaro in Tanzania, which is the highest mountain in Africa reaching 19,341 feet above sea level, ran marathons and completed the Ironman 70.3 Hawaii.

It was the MDS-Marathon des Sables run that pushed Gary out of his comfort zone. This run is a grueling, six-day event in southern Morocco, located in the middle of the Sahara Desert. Many running and extreme enthusiasts consider this race to be the toughest footrace on Earth. Despite the extreme nature of the race, Gary persevered and completed the challenging race.

In reflecting back on the six-day event, Gary felt blessed and energized to be associated with the MDS run because of their service to humanity. The extreme conditions of the event combined with the compassionate nature of the MDS organization provided Gary with an overwhelming sense of pride and accomplishment that he will always feel.

After researching his prestigious biography, I was pleasantly surprised to find out that Gary is also a man of great substance and character. For 25 years, Gary has always championed a cause that promotes the potential of all people, including those with disabilities.

In talking with Gary, it became very clear to me that he is a unique person who believes that teamwork fosters individuality. The historic and record setting event that produced the first ever cross-disability group that successfully reached the Mt. Everest base camp in 2003 is a perfect example. Individually, these brave and inspiring souls would not have been able to conquer the unforgiving and relentless conditions associated with reaching the Mt. Everest base camp; but as a group with a spirited passion and a strategic plan, they obtained a goal, passion and purpose that individually might have been unobtainable.

I learned something else about Gary, too. I had thought that Gary's passion in life was the scaling and conquering of the highest mountain peaks in the world. And while that's true, his true passion and legacy is much more than that. His passion is to continue to empower and motivate individuals to pursue their individual potential. Gary also points out his individual accomplishments in life are purely the groundwork for opportunities that will ultimately promote the potential in humanity as a whole.

Begin your journey

Before we dig in to explore how we can get inspired, we should first delve into why someone would not search for their passion or purpose in life. Simply put, we need to first understand what prevents a person from finding his or her passion.

What is the problem?

Unfortunately, there are too many people in the world that are living in quiet desperation. So many of us get up, go to a job that we don't necessarily like, come home and watch a few hours of TV, go to bed and, of course, we do the exact same thing the next day. Ironically, it is a proven fact that the majority of heart attacks for both men and women occur on Monday mornings between 8 and 9 a.m. during the commute to work. As so many of us can relate to, we dread Sunday evenings and in many cases, begin to feel the anxiety and stress of Monday morning rolling around. The thought of spending yet another day in a mundane, unfulfilling job can literally make a person ill.

Desperation may come in a more subtle form, where one may feel empty and unhappy, or just plain bored with life. Sure, there are fun and happy moments, but mostly we think about the life we wish we were living, even though we don't quite know what that would look like.

> *"The mass of men lead lives of quiet desperation*
> *and go to the grave with the song still in them."*
> *~ Henry David Thoreau*

Many people don't know how to find their passion or purpose in life because they sabotage their search before they even get started. Sabotaging your pending passion in life can arise by accepting everyday circumstances that seem beyond your control. This can make you feel trapped and unable to change course. Sabotaging your passion can often occur simply by choosing to do so. How many of us have yielded to the advice, "That's a pipe dream, give it up and grow up ... nobody gets to have their cake and eat it too".

CHAPTER 2

WHY DON'T PEOPLE PURSUE THEIR PASSION?

Through researching and talking to many people, I have collected the eight most common reasons why individuals do not pursue their passions.

1.) Limiting Beliefs
2.) Anger
3.) Fear of Success
4.) Procrastination
5.) Birds of Feather, flock together
6.) Attitude
7.) Lack of motivation to change
8.) Lack of self-discipline

LIMITING BELIEFS
(Why people don't pursue their passion)
Reason #1

Obstacle One: You don't believe it's possible to find your passion due to limiting beliefs.

We learn our belief systems as very young children and then we move through life creating experiences to match our beliefs.

What is a belief? A belief is a feeling of acceptance through experiences and observations. Past experiences provide the fundamental platform that will determine how you handle and respond to future situations. The challenge is that most of our beliefs are generalizations about our past, based on our interpretations of both painful and pleasurable experiences. Conversely, a limiting belief is a feeling or belief that consciously or subconsciously impedes you from obtaining what you desire.

Examples of Beliefs:
1. We all have beliefs about ourselves, such as *I am a failure,* or, *I am a people person.*
2. We all have beliefs about others, such as *Women should not be in the military,* or, *she is such a kind soul.*
3. We all have beliefs about the world, such as *the people at my job want me to fail,* or, *if you treat others with kindness it will be reciprocated.*

4. We all have beliefs about what is beyond this world, such as God is a kind and understanding being that wants to help us, God has not been fair to me and makes my life difficult, or, there is no God, or God is a part of all of us.

Individuals are not born with a belief system. Your unique belief system is formed, nurtured and cultivated during your early adolescent years through learning, and the observation of your family, social and spiritual environments. After the adolescent years, your belief system has pretty much been formed into a set of core beliefs or as I like to describe them, *guiding principles*. Guiding principals act as the fundamentals that dictate behavior. It is safe to assume that most people do not consciously decide what they are going to believe since beliefs are formed at an early age.

Over the years, everyone begins to acquire limiting beliefs through personal experiences and events. As an example, observing or participating in the negative emotions associated with divorce can nurture the limiting belief that one is not worthy of being in a loving and caring relationship. Due to an unsuccessful relationship, a person may fall into a mental state of self-pity, sorrow and doubt when contemplating future relationships.

Being able to understand what limited beliefs you have acquired over the years can be a process in itself. At some level, limited beliefs can, and will, negatively impact our lives. Some limiting beliefs can be obvious, such as *I'm not good enough, smart enough or attractive enough,* or, *I am too fat, too old, to slow,* are all clearly limiting.

Limiting beliefs can evolve and develop over a period of time and can be somewhat more subtle and difficult to identify." Notice how subtle these limited believes are: *It will be really tough to find a job in this economy,* or, *older people driving cars are simply not good drivers and we need to avoid them.* These judgments and beliefs are still limiting and they will affect our view on events, people and situations.

The reality of a limiting belief is that many of us are not even aware they exist. Unfortunately, when someone has a limiting belief, he or she will not even attempt to embark upon an objective or goal since they have the subconscious belief they will fail. They are hesitant to even try. A man who thinks he's not handsome enough to attract a mate may never even ask for a date. A woman or man who has been divorced can have the belief and emotional feelings that having a loving, caring relationship is impossible for them.

The limiting beliefs that should concern us are those that prevent us from attaining our goals and desires. How do you begin to identify your limiting beliefs? How can you begin to peel back your life to really decipher what limiting beliefs you have formed over the years?

Take a good hard look at yourself and the events in your life that have produced an unhappy outcome. As American businessman and self-help author Tony Robbins says, "You always succeed in producing a result." By that, he means the result you get is exactly the result you produce. It is not a mistake. Consciously or unconsciously, what you obtain is based on what you believe. Truth be told, knowing that you create your results can be empowering! If the results you produce are simply not what you want, there is a limiting belief in play.

For example, your financial picture is a mess. You work really hard and make decent money but you haven't been able to get out of debt. You've cut back expenses, tried budgeting, done everything you can think of but you are still falling farther behind. Or, maybe, you've struggled to get to a healthy weight. You lose a bunch of weight then celebrate by binging and, unfortunately, several weeks later you are right back where you began.

Why are the results not in alignment with what you really want? What area of your life have you really tried to improve but, no matter what, things just didn't get better? Once you ask these questions, you need to take the proactive approach to start the process of unearthing your limiting beliefs and, yes, your limiting decisions. Acknowledging these limited beliefs is a good first step and having a friend or mentor to point out your *belief barriers* can help you reach the realization you may be sabotaging yourself.

You deserve to treat yourself better and to have a fulfilled life that affords you clarity, direction and meaning. Hold yourself and your thoughts to a higher standard and you will begin to see the transformation taking place. After all, you have a long time to spend with yourself, so why wouldn't you aspire to provide fulfillment in your life? Be kind to yourself and have positive thoughts. You are more capable and worthy than you give yourself credit for - take the initiative and believe in yourself.

"The mind is everything. What you think, you become."

~Buddha

Additionally, beliefs can seem to be somewhat self-fulfilling based off an individual's interpretation. For example, since grade school, my friend, Todd, held the belief that he was horrible in sports. In Todd's mind, he genuinely believed that athletics and physical activity were not in his DNA makeup. Todd's internal dialogue was, *"Oh, playing sports and doing physical activity is just too hard. I will never be able to do any sport well anyway, so why do I even bother trying?"* The bottom line is that Todd is already self-defeated before he even tries to play sports. Of course he is going to fail. With this attitude, what chance does Todd have of ever being good at sports or even improving at them at all?

Another example of a limiting belief is found in relationships. Like many people, several of my friends are having relationship issues. Their internal dialogue focuses on their inability to have a lasting relationship. One of my good buddies is convinced that all women are in search of men that have money and great wealth. *"All of the ladies that I have dated have been interested in one thing and one thing only ... money. When I go on a date, the ladies always expect me to pay for everything."* Obviously, these statements are not fair. How can he assume that every date will always be the same? Nevertheless, this is the belief and the mindset of my friend.

> *"The quality of your life is the direct result of the quality of your beliefs."*
>
> ~Essential-Practices

Moving Past Limiting Beliefs

In order for people to move in the right direction and gain control of limiting beliefs, we need to make a basic or "slight" fundamental change in the way we look at barriers or limiting beliefs. The key is to refocus and change our internal dialogue and make the conscious choice of utilizing more positive and reinforcing statements when addressing our limiting beliefs. For example, referring back to Todd, perhaps his internal voice should say: *I bet if I properly prepare myself for an athletic contest or sporting event, I truly believe I could be successful. Or, if I could learn how to catch a ball and practice running like some of the athletes that I see on TV, I eventually could become a very good baseball player.* In other words, changing your mindset and being mentally positive are tremendous first steps in moving past your long held limiting beliefs to move in the right direction.

Maintain a healthy mental disposition

About my negative friend and his misguided belief about women and their sole objective of securing a man who is financially independent and wealthy, perhaps his approach and inner dialogue should sound something like this: *Women, at times, should enjoy the pampering, security and attention that a gentleman can provide. Or, I believe that a woman can also contribute to the financial responsibility for going out to dinner and on vacations.* Once again, this slight and subtle change of attitude can quickly change a negative and condescending mindset into a positive one. That subtle shift toward positivity attracts positivity in others. Soon, Todd would begin to experience more favorable interaction with women in general.

Sometimes people begin the process of finding their passion with serious doubts. They do not believe it is possible. People fundamentally believe life is meant to be difficult and that happiness, clarity and direction are out of their control. However, there is a choice we can make both consciously and subconsciously. We can declare our doubts and limiting beliefs by confronting them and addressing them head on. If we are committed and able to change our ways, we can directly confront the negative and unproductive inner dialogue that lurks within us. People often believe life is meant to be hard and demanding and that rewards are few and far between.

In order to move past these nagging, limiting beliefs, we should look at our limiting beliefs and negative attitudes as wonderful opportunities to expand ourselves and develop into the next area of our growth as productive human beings. The best opportunity for growth, fortitude and self-improvement will emerge when you're facing great adversity in your darkest hour. Our most profound learning experiences as parents, spouses, employees and friends typically come in times of tremendous difficulty when we're under enormous stress. During times of prosperity, bliss, and success, there is not much opportunity for growth since we're celebrating the fruits of our blessings.

I read a terrific story in *Life Success Company*, which is a wonderful organization that talks about limiting beliefs and how important it is to overcome them for our personal development. One poignant article was about how baby elephants in the circus are trained from an early age to stay confined to an area using a thin rope that is wrapped around their ankle. Obviously, the large elephants could break free of the ropes, but they do not due to their limited beliefs they have acquired throughout history. The writer was amazed by this and asked the trainer why these magnificent animals made no attempt to escape. The trainer commented that back when they were young, they used the same-size rope to tie them up and at that age, it was enough to hold them back. As they grow, they are conditioned to believe they cannot break away. They believe the rope can still hold them, so they never try to break free.

These animals could at any time break free from their bonds but because they believed they couldn't, they were stuck right where they were. This powerful and gigantic creature limits its present abilities by the limitations of its past. How many of us go through life believing the same symbolic ropes also bind us?

There were once strong beliefs that the Earth was flat. For many years, this was the common view and belief that if you traveled too far by ship or explored to a certain undisclosed point, you would eventually just fall off the side of the Earth. Of course, this belief was later proved wrong by Christopher Columbus and his historic voyages of the late 1490s. Many beliefs are eventually declared false through scientific data or individual exploration. Limiting beliefs and negative thoughts that have been incorporated into your everyday life will impede you from achieving both your passions and aspirations. Through hard work, dedication, and perseverance, you can prove your limiting beliefs wrong by creating a positive mental shift in your thoughts and actions.

At one point in my life, because I did not have a business degree from college, I was fearful and under the limited belief that I would not be able to get a job or have a career in a business-related field. I believed my Administration of Justice degree was going to limit me to a law enforcement or social services career. This was my internal belief that limited my career choices. In order for me to move past this, I had to initially tell myself that my degree was not a barrier in pursuing a business career. Secondly, I had to take the initiative and actually pursue a business-related job. It can be very difficult to move past a limiting belief but taking the brave step to move out of your comfort zone is the critical first step.

Over the years, I have had conversations with both men and women who were contemplating divorcing their spouses. Infidelity, mental abuse, physical abuse, alcohol abuse, drug abuse, as well as gambling addictions were just some of the reasons why these individuals were seeking divorces. Despite these very serious destructive behaviors, many of the individuals were afraid to part ways from their harmful partners. Financial dependence, emotional ties, children and the same circle of social friends were some of the reasons why these people wanted to stay in the toxic relationships.

Taking the leap of faith and moving outside a comfort zone to end a marriage can be a very difficult undertaking since change is hard and emotionally challenging. To compound the situation, many individuals might have a limiting belief that will make it that much more difficult to end and move past their toxic situation.

Limiting beliefs are self-defeating thoughts that impede us from obtaining something in life that we deem as very important. For whatever reason, these thoughts or learned behaviors will not allow us to take action or responsibility towards our desired goals. The elephants believing they are trapped within the confines of the ropes is actually their internal limited belief. The fact that I felt I was unable to pursue a business career due to my educational background was also a limited belief. Staying in a toxic marriage for all of the wrong reasons is a limiting belief and my friend who believed women were solely in relationships for the financial stability was also a limiting belief. At certain times, your limiting beliefs have shaped your actions. They have prevented you from seeing opportunities and maybe even discouraged you from trying at all. As you can see, living in a situation that is potentially unhealthy and destructive can alter the direction and outcome of your life.

Limiting beliefs or unconscious beliefs can be born from previous painful experiences from early childhood and teenage years that, over a period of time, manifest themselves into a recurring theme of negative and destructive behaviors. These limiting beliefs can become an adaptive measure of our mind. Realizing that earlier experiences can cause us pain, we construct beliefs to avoid those difficult and hurtful situations in our future. Limiting beliefs are also designed to remove responsibility from ourselves. That way, we'll never hurt ourselves again by thinking we can change our situation. It's not that the elephants believe they're too weak, it's that the rope is too strong and therefore they believe there is nothing they can do about it. This mindset can become progressively worse as we become complacent and basically just learn to settle and accept the situation, regardless of the potential ramifications.

Once you believe in your mind that a limiting belief is the truth and this belief becomes solidified and embedded in our brain, we have now entered a phase that is referred to as a self-fulfilling prophecy. Wikipedia describes a self-fulfilling prophecy as a prediction that directly or indirectly causes itself to become true by the very terms of the prophecy itself, due to positive or negative feedback between belief and behavior. Simply stated, you have the ability to fulfill your destiny in life by either positive or negative thoughts. In order to move past these limiting beliefs, it is time to bring these negative beliefs out of hiding and address what they are. You need to be brave and to have the self-discipline, determination and support to move past your limiting beliefs. Once you do that, you have a choice and you can begin the process of pulling in your passion.

"If I want to be free, I have to be me."

– Bob Proctor

The million dollar question is to how you can break through these negative thoughts or pesky devils? Understanding and identifying these limiting beliefs can be an extremely difficult process. Nevertheless, as difficult a task as this might be, it is imperative to go through this process. For example, if you are having trouble finding a relationship, maybe you can justify your situation with something like, *Women only want men who have a lot of money, Guys are only interested in younger women,* or, *I will never be able to live a life of passion. The* bottom line is that anything you say to yourself to rationalize why something isn't working out for you is a limiting belief. Rationalizing or justifying what you say to yourself is the core issue associated with limiting beliefs. Rationalizing is a self-created lie that is communicated by your internal dialogue.

Will that limiting belief sound true to you? Of course! It will sound perfectly reasonable and valid and you probably can come up with lots of evidence to supporting it by rationalization. But, it's still a belief that is getting in the way of what you want. Unless you're willing to totally give up on your goals and desires, it is a limiting decision that you don't want to keep around.

In order for us to break this destructive and negative spiral of non-growth and to move on, we need to attack these limitations head on and break the ropes of our confinement. As we have described, most of us do not consciously decide what we are going to believe. Instead, our beliefs are often misinterpretations of past events. How do ideas turn into beliefs?

One of the most articulate and successful leaders of our generation relating to limiting beliefs is Tony Robbins. He has developed a wonderful way to understand the concept of beliefs and how we expand them into an everyday tool, utilizing them to aid us in developing beneficial beliefs. As Tony suggests, think of an idea like a tabletop with no legs. Without legs, the tabletop won't stand by itself. Belief, on the other hand, has legs. To believe something, you have references to support the idea –specific experiences that back up the belief. These are the legs that give your tabletop the solid foundation that makes you certain about your beliefs.

For example, if you believe you're extremely intelligent, you likely have had many personal life experiences to reinforce that belief. Maybe you did well in school, people always told you how smart you are, or that you caught onto things quickly. You can find experiences to back up almost any belief, both good and bad. The key is to make sure that you're consciously aware of the beliefs you're creating. If your beliefs don't empower you, you will need to change them.

All personal breakthroughs begin with a change in beliefs. The moment we begin to honestly question our beliefs and the experiences we assign to them, we no longer feel absolutely certain about them. This opens the door to replacing your old, disempowering beliefs with new beliefs that support you in the direction that you want to go. If you develop the absolute sense of certainty that powerful beliefs provide, then you can get yourself to accomplish virtually anything, including those things others are certain are impossible.

I wrote that I was blessed to work in a corporate environment for nearly 25 years, working in a multitude of positions relating to sales, marketing and management. Even though I was not making a large sum of money, I earned a good paycheck, drove a company car and was awarded annual bonuses that afforded me the opportunity to take nice vacations with my family. During this time in my life, I felt somewhat content and relatively happy, but in some ways, I felt unchallenged and bored. Basically, I did not feel like I was living up to my potential.

Fast forward several years and always seeking new and exciting ventures, I was offered the opportunity to start a company focusing on real estate development. Back in the mid-1990s, as we all know, real estate was booming and financing was relatively easy. During this time, I resigned from corporate America and dove head first into a full-time entrepreneurial role, acquiring and purchasing mostly commercial properties and land. I also was raising capital venture money to develop

and build-out these promising ventures. For several years, success and the correlating payout was very rewarding financially, but as the old saying goes, all good things come to an end. Indeed, this was my case. During the actual financial recession, I was literally out of business due to the inabilities of the banks to provide commercial financing to prospective buyers.

My financial world turned upside down and my ability to provide food, shelter and clothing for my children became increasingly difficult. As a result of the tremendous financial pressure and other issues, my marriage began to collapse and the family unit that I had been so blessed to have began to fracture in front of my eyes.

Through the next several years, my family's life continued to spiral out of control. During these dark years, I had developed a limiting belief that I was not able to properly provide for my family. Since I had basically lost everything that I had financially, my feeling of self-worth, or lack thereof, was basically at ground zero. As the father, provider and protector to my children, I had formed the limiting belief that I was basically a deadbeat father due to my inabilities to amply provide for my children. In reality, I was still able to provide the basics for my children, but I was very angry with myself since I was not able to sustain the lifestyle to which we had become accustomed.

I had created a limiting belief in my own mind that hindered my worthiness as a father, protector and provider. My limiting belief was that since I wasn't able to provide for my children like I had in the past, I was simply not a good father. This limiting belief was something that I had been carrying with me for some time. Over the last several years, I have been able to move past this limiting belief in both my mind and actions. I have become a stronger father and mentor to my three beautiful children in a different yet more fulfilling and enduring capacity. Even though I can't provide financially like I did before, I was able to replace those legs on the table with more important and meaningful legs. As an example, I am a more patient and caring parent today compared to five years ago. My ability to listen and internalize what my children are communicating to me has improved greatly and in turn, I can offer valuable advice and guidance back to them. Additionally, I have learned to love each and every one of my children for who they are and what they want out of life. Yes, I will continue to mentor and guide them keeping in mind that all children have different talents, likes and dislikes. As parents and mentors, we have to understand these qualities in our children and guide them in the right direction.

Take Full Responsibility for Failures and Non-Acceptance: Do not blame others for your mistakes or setbacks in life and equally important, do not harbor negativity or anger towards individuals or organizations.

Anger and resentment are the devil's way of impeding ones growth and exploration in life. Once you have made the important step of moving in the right direction, it is crucial not to fall back into your past belief patterns, and to also take full responsibility for your past as well as your present situations. If individuals, organizations or potential employers don't accept you or bring you into their world, acknowledge and accept the fact that differences will respectfully exist no matter what you try to do.

> *"Life is 10 percent of what happens to me,*
> *90 percent of how I react to it."*
>
> *- Charles Swindoll*

Changing Your Mindset

The Law of Belief when understood and practiced can help anyone to manifest those events in life that they truly want. Conversely, the law of belief can work the opposite way by attracting negative events and experiences. The trick is that you must first find and release the old belief systems within you before you program yourself with the new. When you want to program the new beliefs then you need absolute clarity on your objectives. You need a solid plan to get you there and then you must believe that you are destined to achieve them. As time passes, you must continuously reinforce your new beliefs. Your positive beliefs, actions and targeted objectives will help you to obtain and realize what your passion in life is.

Since we are all going to be wrong sometimes about certain things we believe, why not choose to overestimate your chances rather than underestimate them? Why not assume you're more than capable rather than less than capable? Why not see yourself as blessed with amazing opportunities instead of a victim who's been screwed over by the world? Both are inaccurate views – or rather, both are subjective views and neither can ever be proven definitively. Making the conscious choice to believe in the success of your actions will provide you the momentum to succeed in life. In your inner dialogue and thoughts, believe that all good will come to you.

You are capable of so much more than you currently think. Why not find evidence that supports THAT belief? Believe that you live a privileged and blessed life already and you don't need anything to prove it to yourself? Believe that you are the best and people will think that you are the best.

Research has shown that people who overestimate their abilities perform better than those who underestimate their abilities. It's not a coincidence that the most successful people in the world tend to be megalomaniacs. Or, as Steve Jobs once said, *"It's the people who are crazy enough to believe they can change the world who do."*

We can easily get stuck in our current existence and make the conscious choice to remain exactly where we are. People don't believe that it is possible to attain their passion or purpose because they are living in their memory, which is based off past experiences that have been learned, observed and reinforced over the years. In this case, people are living life in a robotic fashion representing a reproduction or duplication of their life on a daily basis. In order to move out of this repetitive and non-growth mode, we need to utilize our imagination to visualize what we need to do to advance our lives and discover what our purpose is by simply believing. This process can take a while, but by utilizing your imagination on a regular basis, you will be able to gradually change your fate and slowly begin to cultivate your passion. By visualizing and utilizing your subconscious power via imagination, your purpose in life will begin to take shape.

"Believe in yourself and all that you are. Know that there is something inside you that is greater than any obstacle."
– Christian D. Larson

Overcome Limiting Beliefs

1) *Be a first rate version of yourself:* You owe it to yourself to unearth and act on the strengths and talents that have been bestowed to you. Find out what really drives you and pursue it with a single-mindedness that still leaves room for a well-balanced life.

2) *Dream and go for the goals you set for yourself:* As Les Brown has said, *"Shoot for the moon and if you come up short, you still land into the stars."* Utilize both your mind and imagination to determine your goals.. Visualize them on a regular basis and put a much needed action plan into play.

3) *Challenge and push yourself:* Set the bar high and strive to obtain your desired goal. Once you have made an achievement, continue to press on time and time again.

4) *Trust and love yourself:* You probably spend more time being your own worst enemy instead of being your own best friend. But you deserve to treat yourself better. After all, you have the rest of your life to spend with yourself.

5) *Recall your successes:* Building a platform from your prior successes is a wonderful way to build your future success.

6) *Give yourself permission to try ... and try again:*

Self-doubt or limiting beliefs will never disappear, but you need to be conscious of these life-limiting barriers and avoid them through positive and empowering beliefs. Over time, you keep getting better at dealing with limiting beliefs and learning how to basically ignore them and move on. A limiting belief will greet you every time you fall out of your comfort zone and whenever you strive to do something great.

What You Can Do Today

Four action exercises to immediately help you move past your limiting beliefs.

1) *Find the old non-serving belief systems within you and toss them out.* This requires a lot of honest soul searching to find. It's important to reiterate the question, what is your *belief table*? How can you begin today to build legs onto this table? If your belief table is to be in a strong, loving relationship, you need to build upon the positive events (legs) that you have had in the past relating to relationships. Conversely, take a good hard look at the issues or troubles that you have experienced in the past with relationships. Learn from these and then utilize these lessons as springboards or momentum-lifters to aid in developing new relationships. Make these weaknesses your strengths. Convert these negatives into positives and have them become the legs on your relationship belief table.

2) *Begin to add a "positive belief" system into your life* and start to believe today. Believe that you are destined to be successful in whatever areas you desire. Interestingly enough, once you get a few successes under your belt, your attitude and disposition will begin to change in a positive manner.

3) *As noted, you need to become very clear* and focused on your true desires, make plans to achieve them and believe with absolute conviction that you will achieve them. The universe will conspire to help you achieve it – once you believe it. To help begin this process, utilize your imagination and really dream to help yourself identify what type of visionary goals or passions that you wish to obtain. Make yourself a promise that through your imagination and specific actions plans, you will successfully obtain your passions in life. Be clear and actually write down the promises that you have made to yourself. This will act as a reinforcement tool that will help to hold you accountable.

4) *Get into the habit of acting as though you have already accomplished* your goals and that you are the success you want to be. Your new behaviors will influence your beliefs, which, in turn, will help you to manifest your desires.

Take Action: Focus on the beliefs that will empower you
Belief: *I am very successful financially because I did the following…* This is the table from the earlier example. Listed below are the legs that support the belief table.

-Stayed out of debt for the last 10 years. (leg 1)

-Saved over $10,000 in 4 years (Leg 2).

-Bought a second home back in 2013 (Leg 3)

-(Add legs 4, 5, 6 and 7)

As we add more legs to reinforce our belief table, we slowly begin to create momentum for understanding and enhancing our desired belief.

Belief Systems

Limiting belief systems

For example, *I can't have a good relationship because my parents were not happy and they divorced later in life.* Instead of looking at the negatives relating to not being in a solid relationship, you need to look at your positives and build your *relationship belief table.* Build the relationship belief table on past positive experiences combined with future action plans.

Summary

Limiting beliefs are true barriers that impede your ability to move in the right direction as you begin to relate and identify your passion pursuit. By understanding and conquering self-limiting beliefs, you will be on your way to achieving real potential as a human being. The creative flood gates leading to passion will begin to open! Be brave in your journey and always look at the glass as half-full. Being positive and embracing your life experiences is key to taking your game to the next level.

ANGER
(Why people don't pursue their passion)
Reason #2

"Holding on to anger is like grasping a hot coal with the intent of throwing it at someone else; you are the one who will get burned."

~Gautama Guddha

Dealing with Anger

Anger is a natural emotion and feeling that we have all experienced at some point in our lives and it is the most destructive emotion that a human being can experience. Unresolved anger is one of the chief contributing factors that impedes your ability to identify and pursue your passion. The root cause of anger is tension from past hurts and guilt. It is normal for you to experience anger but be careful not to let this volatile feeling overwhelm you during the occasional bouts when it does happen. Pent up feelings and angry thoughts directed at others or unforeseen events can fester over time and really begin to manifest themselves into resentment and hatred. Resentment and hatred will cloud your common sense and impede your ability to act sensibly.

Many divorced couples experience strong resentment and hostility towards their former partners. Disagreements relating to the financial distributions of assets, issues and conflicts relating to the child custody as well as the overall emotional battering of going through the legal proceedings are just a few of the consequences that drive anger. Over time, the anger can fester and potentially change the makeup and character of a person. Hatred and resentment are serious impediments that will preclude you from unleashing your passion and obtaining your life purpose. Through the entire divorce proceedings that I had with my former wife, like so many divorced couples, I had very strong negative emotions towards her.. The breaking up of the family unit, the allegations and, of course, the ensuing legal battles are all high level stressful events. Don't get me wrong, I was once a willing and able participant in this entire process and I was more than happy to sling mud and fuel the fire of animosity if only because it provided an outlet for anger and retribution. In retrospect, I wish that I would have done things differently for the well-being of my children. Unfortunately, anger and its correlating negative side-effects got the best of me.

Nevertheless, hatred and its close cousin anger are feelings that can really prevent you from being open minded and spirited about finding your passion. When you are feeling hatred in your life, it affects and limits your mental and spiritual openness because you are preoccupied with these past events that have caused you stress and hurtfulness. In order to get past this destructive emotion, you really need to meet it head on so that you can better understand what its driving force is. Being able to understand your anger and frustration is an important first step to take. Why are you mad or angry? Have you been disrespected or put into a situation in which you feel hurt or simply lied to? Is someone grinding down your buttons to the max and making you feel as if you are being used or compromised in some way? In what situations do you feel your anger or hatred start to kick in? What is the driving force that pushes you over the top? All of these questions are valid but you need to do some soul searching to find out the root cause of the anger and how you can learn to cope with it. The first step in moving past anger is simply to be able to let it go and move past the events that have caused it. Dwelling, talking about and rehashing these negative events will only impede your development as an person, which isn't a good thing since every experience offers the potential for growth. I have listed several strategies that will help you to move past anger and resentment.

1) *Surrender Your Ego and Check It At The Door:* Surrendering to your ego's need to always be right and not being spiteful is a key component in moving past your anger. Harboring blame, resentment and being vengeful are not healthy actions in moving past your anger.

2) *Forgiveness:* You need to let go and move on. Forgiving and looking at the glass as half full is a mental shift that needs to happen. Being resentful and holding onto past issues will only hinder your ability to move on. In order to move past anger, we need to learn to forgive or we will continue to experience bouts of anger when our tension-points are triggered.

3) *Learning From The Past:* As we all know, life has it ups and downs. Face it, emotional situations are a fact of life. Learn to take the high road and chalk up past events as learning experiences, which will ultimately help you to grow and mature as a person.

4) *Avoid Knee Jerk Reactions:* Post anger events and emotions can easily be triggered by certain events. Being mindful and aware of these explosive potential situations is imperative. More importantly, if you find yourself getting pulled into a volatile situation that has caused you anger in the past, do yourself a favor and immediately try to defuse the situation by simply walking away. Be the better person. As you have learned already, by confronting or addressing the situation head on, like a bull in a china shop, you are only throwing gas on the fire, which will resurrect past anger and emotions.

5) *Relaxation & Exercise:* Over the years, I have incorporated a breathing regimentation that can help you to stay calm in stressful situations. Utilizing deep breathing techniques combined with relaxing thoughts will help to soothe hostile and angry feelings. Going to the gym is also a healthy way to channel frustration and anger. Take your frustrations out on the heavy bag, do some extra sets on the bench press, or climb on the treadmill and start running. When you work out and utilize breathing techniques, your body will naturally produce and release endorphins. Endorphins are natural opiate-like hormones that are produced in the human body. The release of these chemicals will act as a natural antidepressant that will help to calm you and make you more relaxed.

FEAR OF SUCCESS
(Why people don't pursue their passion)
Reason #3

"The worst enemy to creativity is self-doubt."

– Sylvia Plath

In an interesting article was published by Gilbert Williams entitled "The Path," Mr. Williams describes how often we have heard about our fear of failure. In contrast, it was also presented about a decade ago as this revelatory understanding that there is also a fear of success. Over the last decade, this phrase has generated momentum and clarity, which has shed considerable light on it. Many people have come to realize that the fear of success is actually more powerful than the fear of failure. You have learned through conditioning, from the time you were a child, to cope with failure. Like most people, we are prepared to deal with failure but not necessarily success.

Some people are afraid they will fail or even worse, that they may actually succeed in life. With this mindset, you wouldn't even bother trying to attain a goal or to identify your passion because of the consequences associated with success. Furthermore, you would lack belief in yourself and in your potential. Embracing this self-defeatist attitude, you would think if you fail, everyone will think negatively of you. Conversely, if you succeed in an endeavor, people will be envious and think negatively of you. As you can plainly see, this becomes a lose-lose situation no matter how you look at it. Like fear, joy and sadness, self-doubt is part of human nature and it needs to be understood. If you want to improve yourself, you need to tame your self-doubt, not fight with it.

Surprisingly enough, experts have noted that success is much more complex than failure. On some level, it's more comfortable to stay in a familiar situation, even if it doesn't feel great on the surface. But achieving success (however you define it) means you are entering uncharted territory, which, in itself, can be frightening. You are putting yourself out there to be scrutinized, perhaps even criticized, and exposing yourself to new pressures and demands.

Human nature dictates that it is perfectly normal to wonder if you will be up for the challenge of success. Perhaps a part of you would simply rather not take the risk for a number of reasons. Although the idea of success can be daunting, the reality is generally easier to cope with than what you had before. The belief is that if you have been able to keep yourself going during the difficult times then you should be able to be resourceful and keep yourself going during the good times.

Overcoming Fear

1) *Start By Acknowledging It.* Be honest about understanding exactly what your fear is. It's easy to ignore or deny our fears or successes, even to ourselves, in a society and culture that stresses the importance of being strong and brave. By addressing and admitting to your feelings of fear or success, you have taken the crucial first step to gain control over any situation. Once you have acknowledged this, you need to begin to define the specifics associated with it. When did this fear start and how has it been affecting you over the years? Why are we concerned with our potential success in our new career? When you have identified the fear, write it down. Face it head on! Next, explain the details of how the fear began. But don't put the pen down yet. Conversely, writing the success down will help you to begin the visual process of what you're up

against. Talking with others that have witnessed your successes will be a good resources for you because these people can shed light and understanding. That, in turn, can help you deal with any current situation. Also, talking to others can help you identify your fear.

Case Scenario: To help you limit your fear or better yet, understand it before it actually happens, try this exercise.

a) Think about your vision and goals and write then down.

b) Now write down all the things that you are afraid of if you throw yourself head first into the situation. Allow yourself to experience the fear while you write these things down. For instance, *What if I embarrass myself? What if I get fired? What if my wife leaves me? What if I go broke?*

Once you have identified the *What if* scenarios, you need to begin to create a vision and transform each *What if* into a potential positive outcome.

What if I embarrass myself... and at least I can say that I tried, and I can learn from my experience and build from that.

In summary, we need to turn or redirect every *what if* into a positive and position it as a *what could be* created instead. Please remember that all visions and goals come with some type of fear or risk factor. In order to pursue and unleash your passion in life, you need to assume some risk and step outside of your comfort zone.

2) *Own it:* Take responsibility and ownership for your fear. Be truthful with yourself and own up to the fact that it is your fear because many times we tend to blame others or "circumstances beyond our control" for the fear we are experiencing. Fear is an emotion that takes you out of your comfort zone because it represents the unknown. Once you are able to take responsibility for your fears, you can begin to own the fact that YOU are the only one who can change them. Once you realize and acknowledge this, you are on the powerful path to moving beyond fear. Fear of success and fear of failure are all related to being taken out of your comfort zone. In order to get past this, an initial first step is to actually visualize the awesome success that you want. This will help you to begin preparing for, accepting and moving past our fear.

Accept What You Don't Know

Often, your fear lies in the unchartered waters that you are currently navigating through in your life. Please take comfort in the fact that we all fear the unknown. At one point in my professional career, I had started a new career with a Fortune 100 company. This organization was the world's largest financial institution. It was aggressively buying and devouring other banks at lightening speed. Like many newcomers that had made the commitment to get back into the structure of corporate America, I was nervous before my actual start date. You know the feeling that you sometimes get in the pit of your stomach? I had to think about where it was coming from. As you will recall, I had been an entrepreneur for the previous 10 years and just the anticipation of working again in the stodgy, oppressive corporate environment and the structure that this represented had me in knots.

In order for me to address and understand my fears, I needed to learn and build my capabilities relating to that unknown aspect associated with my new job. Like a new college student embarking upon their first job or a stay-at-home mother who hangs up her jeans and again braves the icy waters of corporate America, all of us deal with the anxiety and stresses associated with change at some time or another. In order to help with transitioning into a new phase of life, you need to ask questions and be open minded about new ventures that you are pursuing.

Be brave. Be bold. Walk into the unknown with your eyes wide open. Look at this new adventure as if you are walking into a dark room. Initially, you feel scared and don't know what to expect but once you turn the light on, everything gets clear and simple. On a personal note, I have been able to channel my fears and uncertainties about change into a positive, constructive activity that has enabled me to grow and expand in profound ways, professionally, socially and intellectually.

PROCRASTINATION
(Why people don't pursue their passion)
Reason #4

*"Procrastination is the bad habit of putting off until
the day after tomorrow what should have been
done the day before yesterday."*

~Napoleon Hill

Procrastination is the most expensive invisible cost associated with a business in the modern day business world. The impact of procrastination to the individual from both a professional and personal point of view is quite alarming. According to Gallup polls, on the average, the American worker will procrastinate an average of two hours per day. If you do the math, that can really add up. Assuming the average employee earns $20 an hour, this represents an annual cost to employers of nearly $10,500 per year, per employee.

In fact, studies indicate that 84 percent to 86 percent of people procrastinate on a regular basis. Out of those, a staggering 20 percent of those people chronically avoid difficult tasks and deliberately look for distractions. Look around your house or any place of business and you will find plenty of distractions. The internet, interoffice gossiping, texting, watching TV and just plain being lazy are the main contributors to workforce and individual procrastination. Procrastination, or the inability to focus on the task at hand because you are willfully distracting yourself, is one of the most self-defeating behaviors of a creative person. This, in turn, contributes to your inability to identify and pursue your passion. It's another stumbling block you have created without even knowing it. A vicious cycle of anxiety, stress and more procrastination can be hard to break. Psyblog, "understanding your mind" categorized the five main "thieves of time":

1) *The Busy Bees:* Some people are always busy with tasks related and unrelated to the business at hand. They are always running around doing everything else other than the things they are supposed to do. They are people that fail to understand the difference between *doing the right things* and *doing the things right.*

2.) *Just plain Lazy:* Unlike the busy bee, some folks are like molasses in winter. They exhibit no sense of urgency or willpower. Therefore, you may ask, how do they get anything done? Overall, these individuals are not motivated to take the initial first step. The answer is that all too often they don't accomplish anything positive.

3) *Time Waster:* The time waster simply wastes time by avoiding the task that needs to be addressed. For whatever reason, they choose to divert the time and attention necessary to tackle the matter at hand. Lack of focus and commitment combined with poor time management are the main characteristics of this individual.

4) *Analyzer:* As the name suggests, this group of procrastinators will spend lots of time analyzing the tasks or duties on hand. Analysis by paralysis is the motto here. Simply not taking action is the analyzer's way of dealing with what needs to be done.

5) *Lack of Prioritizing:* This procrastinator is a combination of many of the aforementioned individuals. The main issue is that without prioritizing the tasks that are the most important in a logical or systematic fashion, things rarely done.

Overcome procrastination in the workforce and in life

As with any weakness, the first step you need to take in addressing your procrastination issue is to be upfront and honest with yourself in exploring what exactly your weakness is. Once you understand what your weakness is, you need to implement an ongoing strategy to handle your weaknesses. Some practical tips to avoid unproductive procrastination are as follows:

1) *Take your work seriously.* Set working hours that may not be disturbed or interrupted, whether it is an hour or 10 hours a day. Avoid social networking, texting, folding laundry, computer games, and anything that distracts you during these critical, productive times. Utilizing a daily calendar highlighting specific tasks in correlation with specific times is a valuable step in keeping yourself focused on your objective.

2.) *E.B. White said,* "A writer who waits for ideal conditions under which to work will die without putting a word on paper." In other words, don't wait for the perfect time to work or to explore action plans to pursue your passions. The time is at hand. It's right now! Work consistently even if it is under conditions that might not be necessarily ideal. As an athlete for 23 years of my life, to me athletics and life in general are ripe with many parallels. In athletics, times of improvement and growth occur when you are tired, stressed and under the proverbial gun. Think of the conditions that you work under stress or fatigue. During these trying and difficult times, you will evolve as an athlete, a performer, and a better human being.

"A writer who waits for the ideal condition under which to work will die without putting a word on paper."
~ *E.B.White*

In life, times of difficulty and hardship will help you to grow as a person and as an individual. Let's face it, when life is easy and everything is falling into place, our development as a person is not necessarily in growth mode. Conversely, times of adversity, difficulties and challenge will stretch us in ways we never thought possible. Your growth as a human being through times of adversity is astounding.

3) *Do not wait for the perfect time* to begin the process of unleashing your passion. Begin today! Take the proactive steps to fulfill your goals and aspirations in life. Procrastination and putting off until tomorrow what can be accomplished today only results in an unfulfilled life. Make today, this very moment, the perfect time to unleash your passion.

4) *Obtaining your goals and aspirations in life* can be frighteningly daunting in nature. Do yourself a favor by breaking your work into manageable pieces. As author Gretchen Rubin reminds us, "We tend to overestimate what we can do in a short period of time, and underestimate what we can do over a long period, provided we work slowly and consistently." Additionally, Penn State Football Coach Joe Paterno reminded us that, "If you take care of the little things daily, the big things will take care of themselves down the road." If you make the decision to procrastinate or practice being unproductive, you are telling yourself that texting or washing the dishes is more important than expressing yourself creatively in a form that you can share with the world. Quiet your inner voice of doubt relating to being unproductive and believe in yourself by allowing your creative nature and actions to kick into high gear. Only then, will you speed towards achieving your goals.

5) *Make promises to yourself relating to your goals and objectives.* When setting a goal or working diligently to hurdle a milestone, reposition your objectives as if they are actual promises that you are making to yourself. Hold yourself accountable. Write your promises down so that you can visually identify what you have promised. Then, revisit your accountability worksheet on a daily basis. Remember, small, gradual steps will lead to major successes down the road. Keep the faith soldier and in the words of Phi Gamma Delta, always remember and utilize the Greek term *Perge*.

BIRDS OF FEATHER, FLOCK TOGETHER
(Why people don't pursue their passion)
Reason #5

"If you hang out with chickens, you're going to cluck.
If you hang out with Eagles, you're going to fly."
                                        ~Steve MarAboli

One of the main factors relating to your success or failure can be directly related to the people that you surround yourself with. When you hang out with toxic people that always want to bring you down, prove you wrong and complain about everything, your attitude changes and you will start to see life in a negative manner. Negative individuals will poison your mind. Their state of hopelessness will drag you down into their belief system. Negative thoughts are like Miracle Grow for fear and self-doubt. After 25 years of research, Dr. David McClelland of Harvard University concluded that the choice of a negative "reference group" was in itself enough to condemn a person to failure and underachievement in life. Your associations in life will be the most important factors in determining who you become and what you accomplish in your life.

If you hang out with pessimistic people who are critical of you, their negative comments will likely impact how you view your abilities, your self-image and ultimately, hinder your ability to pursue your passion.

"You will become the combined average of five people that you hang around the most. You will have their combined attitude, health and income."

~ *Jim Rohn*

I can assure you that Jim Rohn's statement is true. You become like those whom you associate with. How can you utilize Jim's quote to your advantage? It's simple. If you want to advance your life personally and professionally, you must associate with at least five people who will be a positive influence in your life. Surrounding yourself with five positive, sincere and motivating individuals will provide you with a springboard to truly achieve in life.

The number five is the pivotal point that will help define your life and what lies on the road ahead. It is imperative for you to focus your attention on the number five because having associations are like elevators - some will take you up and some will take you down. Finding five friends that aspire to achieve goals similar to yours is a good starting number to have. Conversely, you probably have friends that take your attitude down because they are always complaining, blaming, judging or just having a bad attitude. We all know people like this. Right? These negative people do not support your ideas or innovative thoughts. Typically, they downplay and minimize your creative nature and drown out your inner passionate person.

Do you want to surround yourself with these types of people? Or, would you prefer to surround yourself with an overachiever that can empower, encourage and expand your ideas. As common sense dictates, we want to associate and align ourselves with individuals that will expand and support our ideas. These core friends will help elevate your thinking, ideas, vision, dreams and support your commitment to unleashing your passion by taking your life to the next level.

"Great minds talk about ideas, average minds talk about events and small minds talk about people."
~Unknown

Once you make the choice to identify and associate yourself with more positive people, you also become more positive with a solid outlook, which will ultimately change your mental disposition in a productive fashion. We all know, for obvious reasons, as we get older making friends will slow down. Working 60 hours a week, getting married, having children as well as taking on other responsibilities will obviously hinder your ability to form new friendships. As people approach midlife, the days of youthful exploration have pretty much dissipated. As schedules compress and priorities change, may find you're not forming new relationships. Since you're likely to grow closer to your existing network of friends take pause and think about a few things.

Some Important Steps to Take

1) If you want to be more successful, you have to start hanging out with more successful people. If you are unable to physically hang around successful people, utilize the tremendous resources that are available via the internet. YouTube is an internet resource that I have personally used for several years that affords me the opportunity to connect and observe key people that I want to be associated with.

2) If you want to be in the greatest shape of your life, you have to start hanging out with people who are in better shape than you.

3) If you are an employee and you want to become an entrepreneur, you have to start hanging out with other entrepreneurs.

As a young athlete growing up in suburban Philadelphia, I was very active in sports. It just happened by coincidence that I played with other kids and athletes that were older and stronger than me. My older sister, Pam, didn't mind me hanging out with her friends, which gave me the opportunity to train with more mature and seasoned student-athletes. Since I played sports with the older athletes, I also became a better athlete. I can vividly remember getting pummeled into the ground by the older kids. By the time I entered high school, I was an accomplished athlete thanks to my training with, and pummeling by, the older jocks. The point is that by associating and being with older athletes that could push me both physically and mentally at very high levels, I was able to raise my bar of excellence to be the best that I could be. I went on to earn a full football scholarship to Penn State University. By simply associating and hanging out with a peer group that gives you the support, encouragement, disciplinary structure and empowerment to do well in life, you will increase your chances in becoming a productive, open-minded person with the inner strength to attack your purpose in life.

In other words, when you associate with others who have a greater skill set or have achieved more, you are challenged and often motivated to take initiative. It will brings out the best in you and inspire progress and growth in your own life. Observing and modeling someone's positive example will help you reach new heights. I'm not just talking about sports or games but more importantly, I am talking about life and career choices. Sure, you are born into your family. Of that, you have no choice. But you do have a conscious choice to pick your sphere of influence from a different social and professional pool.

Whether you evaluate your current friends, or look to gather more appropriate friends, ask yourself if they can help to improve your quality of life?

Evaluating a friend

1) Do you want to spend more time with them because they make you feel good?

2) Are you motivated to want to be better after you talk to them?

3) Do you feel uplifted after a conversation with them?

ATTITUDE
(Why people don't pursue their passion)
Reason #6

What's Your Attitude?

"Keep your thoughts positive because your thoughts become your words. Keep your words positive because your words become your behavior. Keep your behavior positive because your behavior becomes your habits. Keep your habits positive because your habits become your values. Keep your values positive because your values become your destiny."

– Mahatma Gandhi

What a wonderful saying by the Indian leader Gandhi and how relevant it is in today's environment. One of the most important steps you can take to achieve your greatest potential in life is to learn to monitor your attitude. Evaluate its impact and on your work performance and your relationships with everyone around you.

Failure is the highway to success. As Tom Watson Sr. so aptly stated, "If you want to succeed, double your failure rate." If you study history, you will find that all stories of success are also stories of great failures. But people don't see the failures. They only see one side of the picture and they say that person was both tenacious and lucky - "He, or she, must have been at the right place at the right time."

Let me share someone's life history with you. This was a man who had already failed in business by the age of 21, he was defeated in a legislative race at age 22; failed again in business at age 24; overcame the death of his sweetheart at age 26 then had a nervous breakdown at age 27. If you think any of that stopped him from plowing forward, you're quite mistaken. He went on and lost a congressional race at the age of 34. Did he give up? Not a chance. He then went on to lose a senatorial race at age 45; failed in an effort to become vice-president at age 47; lost a senatorial race at age 49; and was elected president of the United States at age 52.

This man was Abraham Lincoln. We obviously would not call Abraham Lincoln a failure. Instead, most people call Lincoln a great success based on his achievements and positive attitudes to obtain his goals in life.

People often don't realize that they have a choice relating to attitude. You can choose an inner dialogue of self-encouragement and self-motivation, or you can choose one of self-defeat and self-pity. You have the power! It's your choice. At certain points in our life's experience difficult times, heartache as well as physical and emotional pain. The key is to learn from this is that it's not what happens to you that matters, but how you choose to respond to it.

As the father of three beautiful daughters, I have been truly blessed. They are intelligent, ingrained with a solid work ethic and in most cases, the young ladies exercise good, common sense. My one daughter, for whatever reason, sometimes has a negative-Nellie attitude. Her outlook on life can be dismal and her interaction with me can be negative and somewhat condescending. As a parent, this can be annoying but as you may know, teenagers will be teenagers and being a parent is NOT an easy endeavor. In trying to be a good parent, I am constantly reminding my child to have a better attitude.

"Be thankful for what you have and don't look at what you don't have," I tell her. "You have been blessed to have both your health and opportunity in this great country that we live in. Just be thankful". Of course my child raises her eyes as she reluctantly listens to the advice and guidance from her *old man*.

As with my daughter and as well as many people, they have to make the conscious choice to cultivate and bring out their inner dialogue relating to being positive. Having an internal spirit that cultivates self-encouragement and self-motivation will help you to manifest a positive aura that will be felt by those around you. In other words, you need to have a positive attitude and it comes from within.

Think about your attitude as a type of computer that can be self-programmed via your inner voice and self-beliefs. As a youngster, your mind is programmed to think in either a productive or unproductive fashion. Internally, your inner dialogue is the driving force that programs your attitude that, in turn, represents how you present yourself to the world around you. Whether the information is right or wrong, negative or positive, we're programmed as children. Think about what's been programmed into you. It was fed to you through verbal, physical, observation or events. Unfortunately for those who received negative signals, they will continue to hear and feel them for many years.

Do not linger in the past. That isn't always as easy as it sounds, is it? Like the tortoise who plodded on to overcome the hare, it is imperative that you move on with your life. The loudest and most influential voice you hear is your own inner voice, your self-critic. Let that voice be your driving force, drowning out all others. It can work for, or against, you depending on the message that you allow yourself to send. It can be optimistic or pessimistic. It can lift you up or break you down but only you can consciously take the responsibility for the conversation.

"Your attitude, not your aptitude, will determine your altitude."
– Zig Ziglar

Steve Under Fire: A Positive Attitude Saved His Life

When you stare into the barrel of a gun, life probably doesn't seem so rosy. But somehow, Steve managed to make it through what was undeniably one of the most horrific days of his life.

When I first met Steve, before he was shot, I thought to myself, *He's the quintessential guy you love to hate.* He was always in a good mood and always had something positive to say. When someone would ask him how he was doing, he would reply, "If I were any better, I would be twins!"

Steve's a popular restaurant manager both with employees and customers. He is a natural motivator, the kind of person that draws you in with his warmth and good nature. You've heard the adage about making lemonade when life throws you lemons. Well, if Steve owned the restaurant it would serve a lot of lemonade!

"Life is all about making the right choices," Steve says. "Yes, you will sometimes make the wrong choice but learn to understand why you made the wrong choice and move on. When you cut away all the junk, every situation is a choice. You choose how you react. You choose to be in a good mood or bad mood. The bottom line: It's your choice how to live life."

What Steve didn't know was that his philosophy would be put to the ultimate test. He would have to choose between life and death. He chose to live.

One day, when Steve was at the restaurant alone he left the back door open to let a breeze in. Unfortunately, the breeze wasn't the only thing that came through the back door. Three men entered brandishing weapons. When Steve was ordered at gunpoint to open the safe, his trembling hands couldn't spin the dial accurately. With each failed attempt the robbers became increasingly impatient, which skyrocketed into anger.

The unthinkable happened when one of the three thieves panicked and pulled the trigger. Frightened and now yelling at one another, the three men ran off as Steve lay bleeding on the floor.

Luckily, a cook came to work soon after and Steve was quickly rushed to the local trauma center. After 18 hours of surgery and weeks of intensive care, Steve was released from the hospital with bullet fragments still lodged inside his body.

When I asked him months later how he was, Steve replied, "If I were any better, I'd be twins. Do you want to see my scars?" I declined. But I couldn't believe my ears. Incredulously I asked him, after being shot, how he could still have a positive attitude?

"The first thing that went through my mind was that I should have locked the back door, " Steve replied jokingly. "Then, as I lay on the floor, I remembered that I had two choices. I could choose to live, or I could choose to die. I chose to live."

"Weren't you scared? I asked.

"The paramedics kept telling me I was going to be fine but when they wheeled me into the emergency room and I saw the expressions on the faces of the doctors and nurses, I got really scared," Steve admitted. "In their eyes, I read, 'He's a dead man.' I knew that I needed to take action."

"What did you do?" I asked.

"Well, there was a big nurse shouting questions at me," Steve said. "She asked if I was allergic to anything. 'Yes' I replied. The doctors and nurses stopped working as they waited for my reply. I yelled, 'Bullets!' Over the laughter, I told them,

"Look, I am choosing to live. Operate on me as if I am alive, not dead."

Steve lived thanks to the skill of his doctors and because of his conscious choice to live. Like Steve, every day you have the choice to live fully. Make your choice on the positive side. Face the sun and leave the dark shadows stay behind you.

The Power of Positive Thinking - Making the Choice

In life, we have the choice when we wake up in the morning to have either a positive disposition or a negative one. Positive thinking is a mental and emotional attitude that focuses on the bright side of life and expects positive results.

A positive person anticipates happiness, health and success, and believes he or she can overcome any obstacle. Health and Fitness writer Leanne Beattie notes that happiness may be attained through positive self-talk. She points out that being an optimist or a pessimist boils down to the way you talk to yourself.

"Optimists believe that their own actions result in positive things happening, that they are responsible for their own happiness, and that they can expect more good things to happen in the future."

A true optimist will not blame themselves when bad things happen. Typically, they view bad events as a result of something outside of themselves. I didn't blame myself for losing my job, but saw it as a business decision that had nothing to do with me personally." In my opinion and generally speaking, optimistic people view themselves as positive and more confidently than pessimistic people.

Beattie continues by saying, "Pessimists think the opposite way. They blame themselves for the bad things that happen in their lives and think that one mistake means more will inevitably come."

My experience with pessimists is that even though they may have a negative Nellie attitude, they can still be successful in life and often are. As funny as it sounds, there can be effective pessimists that will systematically hedge their bets against the odds and still come out positive.

Contrasting Mindsets: Negative vs. Positive

Negative Mindset: Remez Sasson authored a nice article entitled, "The Power of Positive Thinking" that simplifies how you can look at positive thinking in contrast to negative thinking and the correlating end result.

Allan applied for a new job, but he didn't believe that he would get it since his self-esteem was low. He considered himself a failure and unworthy of success because he believed that success and accomplishments were outside of his scope.

As you can see, Allan has a pessimistic view towards himself. His overall attitude and belief system was negative towards himself and he therefore believed that other applicants were better and more qualified than him. Allan's mind was worked overtime on developing negative thoughts and fears concerning the job the entire week preceding the job interview. In reality, Allan actually anticipated and projected failure and disappointment.

On the day of the interview, Allan woke up late and, to his horror, he discovered that the shirt he planned to wear was dirty, and his other one needed ironing. As it was already too late, he went out wearing a wrinkled shirt and skipping breakfast. Due to Alan's lack of preparation and his negative attitude, he not only came across during the interview as intensely negative, but he was preoccupied with worrying about his shirt. All this distracted his mind and made it difficult for him to focus on the interview. His overall behavior made a bad impression and consequently, he materialized his fear and lack of preparation internally and unfortunately, Allan did not get the job.

"Whatever the mind can conceive and believe it can achieve."
– Napoleon Hill

Positive Attitude: Eye of the Tiger

Jim applied for the same job but approached the interview process in an upbeat and optimistic fashion. He was sure that he was going to get the job. During the week preceding the interview, he often visualized and mentally programmed himself to make a good impression and getting the job. Preparing and getting familiar with the anticipated questions prior to the actual interview gave Jim a sense of comfort and ease. The evening before the interview, he prepared the clothes he was going to wear, and went to sleep a little earlier. On the day of the job interview, Jim woke up earlier than usual, had ample time to eat breakfast and then to arrive to the interview before the scheduled time. As you can imagine, Jim made a good impression and got the job.

The stories serve to illustrate the fact that having a positive attitude and preparing for an important event will help you to achieve your desired outcome.

Positive Thinking

When we make the conscious choice of having a positive attitude, we will experience the following:

Happiness, energy and a spring in our step. Positive thinking will show in your body language. Having an optimistic disposition will help you to exude confidence, happiness and a sense of good will. A natural by product of positive thinking and actions will result in you simply feeling better about yourself and your surroundings.

Practical Instructions for Positive Thinking

I must admit, it's easy to preach about having a positive attitude. Following through with that advice can be difficult at best. As I have learned via the school of hard knocks, inner work and self-realization are required in order to implement positive change in your life. Attitudes and thoughts do not change overnight. But the result of your tenacious efforts will be a more passionate, fulfilled you.

In order to begin the process of positive thinking, you should really think long and hard about its benefits and persuade yourself to try. The power of your positive thoughts and actions can help to shape your life. The shaping process can be done subconsciously, but it is possible to make the process a conscious one. Visualizing and believing that you can make this fundamental change is the key. As many of you are thinking, this may seem somewhat strange, but nevertheless, give it a try. You have nothing to lose and everything to gain. To reiterate, if you want to change your life, you have to do things differently or you will continue down the same road day in and day out. And frankly, you wouldn't be reading this book if you didn't want to unlock the cage to unleash your inner passion. The golden key to your future is in your hand.

Sometimes blazing a new path can be difficult and lonely for anyone who makes a decision to change. If you have friends and associates that are not supporting your new beliefs, ideas and thoughts, you might want to rethink your core social network.

> *"Utilize your imagination to visualize your*
> *new found thoughts and beliefs."*
> *- Unknown*

In addition to using positive words in your inner dialogue, let them flow freely when talking to others. And don't forget about your body language. Nonverbal communication conveys to the world your inner positive passion, confidence and strength. Simple things like smiling and good posture help to reinforce positive thoughts, which will ultimately develop a strong framework that will enable you to pursue your passion and purpose. Sit up straight in your chair and smile! This is a simple step to begin transitioning towards a positive mental mindset.

A negative thought can wipe a smile off of your face faster than a zookeeper can slam a tiger's gate shut. Be proactive by replacing negative thoughts with positive ones. If the negative thought returns, replace it again with a positive one. Imagine yourself looking at two pictures. Now, choose the one that makes you happy because this is you giving yourself positive reinforcement. Persistence and training will eventually teach your mind to think positively and to ignore negative thoughts. In case you experience inner resistance and difficulties when replacing negative thoughts with positive ones, do not give up, but keep looking only at the positive picture you have created. You are the one that prevents the zookeeper from shutting the cage door.

It doesn't matter what your circumstances are at the present time. Think positively, expect only favorable results and the correlating circumstances will change accordingly. If you persevere, you will transform the way your mind thinks. It might take some time for the changes to take place, but eventually they will. Small, gradual steps of success created by your new positive outlook will inspire you to leap into your passionate future.

Developing a Winning Attitude

Bad attitudes are typically the result of past experiences and events. It is very challenging to change your habitual bad attitudes since many people let them become a part of their DNA. You might want to ask yourself if you have allowed past experiences to affect your attitude negatively? Negative attitudes are similar to limited beliefs in the sense that these destructive behaviors can impede you from obtaining your passion or purpose in life.

Common causes that I have discovered that drive a bad attitude include low self-esteem, stress, fear, resentment, anger, hopelessness and an inability to handle change. It can take a lot of effort to identify the root causes of bad attitudes but through hard work, dedication (and if need be psychological counseling and guidance) you can conquer what is restraining you and empower yourself to move to the next level. As you can imagine, by defeating and moving past negative attitudes, you can finally eliminate excess baggage from your life, which will help you to begin the process of developing a better attitude and ultimately, help you to begin the process of unleashing your passion.

Being Proactive and Changing Your Attitude

Changing your attitudes can have an extremely beneficial impact on your life. Several of the idea's below are from Justin Riggs article from Tiny Buddha, "simple wisdom for complex lives."

> *1) Turn negative situations* into positives ones. Sound difficult? It's not. Simply learn to appreciative what surrounds you: I absolutely love this quote from Les Brown, who said that, "The issues and problems that we are faced with in life are God's way of cleverly providing us with wonderful opportunities." Simply stated, don't dwell on negative issues and events in life, just look at them as temporary situations that will pass. Ultimately, these situations enable you to learn and grow. Les' very powerful passage needs to be internalized, digested and understood.

2) Philanthropist and founder of Templeton Mutual Funds Sir John Templeton also noted that appreciating what is around you is a positive component of life. "An attitude of gratitude creates blessings," John writes. Bearing that thought in mind, everyday you should look for things to be grateful for despite how tough life may appear on the surface. I can guarantee you that there are many people in the world that are suffering way beyond the pains and inconvenience that you are going through so, please, be grateful for what you have and start the day with a positive mind set. You will not allow the cage door to be closed.

3) *Change your beliefs by controlling your thoughts* and the way you digest information. Start with some of your negative beliefs like, "I am not good at working with computers or I am socially awkward at times." This thought process or mind set is blocking your success. In your mind, turn that negative thought into a positive, reinforced one by saying, "I enjoy working with computers or hey, I like being in a social setting ... especially when I try and apply myself." If you keep talking to yourself and visually seeing yourself act in that manner, you will begin to gradually change and you will see the transformation happen in front of you. Keep reinforcing your positive thoughts through visualization and actions. Believe in yourself and keep your thoughts, actions and associations positive with strong beliefs and an upbeat attitude.

4) *Think before you react.* We all have trigger situations that propel us into a bad mood, which gives us a bad attitude towards life. As I am sure you know, it is not the event, experience or problem itself that causes the stress. It is the way we respond to it that makes us feel the way we do. For example, I sometimes get overwhelmed on the weekends because of the countless hours that I spend driving my three children around to different activities, friend's houses, shopping malls and other places. It's like the zookeeper has a whip that's being used to send me in a chosen direction with no regard to my own thoughts and desires. In the past, I would have gotten stressed and lost my temper with the time requirements that I had to commit to in order to fulfill my children's rigorous social responsibilities. Today, I reflect and look inwardly and embrace the reliance that my children demand of me. I cherish these moments and look at them as wonderful opportunities to further connect with my darling off-springs in a compassionate and fulfilled manner. By simply looking at our commitments and demands in a different light, we can quickly change our attitudes and outlook into something very positive.

From Negative to Positive

1) *Keeping your priorities in line.* We all experience stress and bad days at the office. It's the nature of the Corporate Beast. Corporate goals, financial deadlines, after hour conference calls and 60-hour plus workweeks can transform the best of people into the craziest of beasts. What good does it do to take your frustrations, stress, and resentments home after work? Leave your work problems, headaches, issues and concerns at work. That's one cage door you can and should close at the end of the work day.

Make yourself a promise; before you walk into your home to greet your loved ones, do clear your head in a way that enables you to leave your work problems at work. Go for a run, take a walk or simply go to the gym to clear your mind and body of toxins from work. Remember, get clear on the consequences of your bad attitude and don't forget you could be hurting the one's closest to you. Be the bigger person and utilize a mature restraint before you lash out at the ones that are looking to you for guidance and direction.

2) *Be Happy:* Remember the song, "Be Happy"? What a great song to hang your happy hat on. No matter what the situation is, just be happy. The theme of the song is basically just to be happy with who you are and what you have now, no matter what the situation. The song itself has a Reggae vibe that has a carefree nature in both the words and rhythm. Sipping an ice cold Corona beer on the beach while watching the ocean wave's crash is the visual mindset that created by the rhythm and melody. What did I take from the song that you should to? Don't take life too seriously and don't sweat the small stuff. If you have a smile on your face and a positive disposition, all will be well. So relax, sit back and have a Corona.

3) Develop your positive attitude with regular, repetitive positive thoughts. In general, I look at myself as a positive person. Obviously, nobody is perfect and as many people will tell me, especially my children and finance, I am far from being perfect. Nevertheless, I am constantly trying to modify, change and perfect my ability to enhance my good natured and positive attitude. This can be difficult at times as life and its everyday occurrences can always throw us a curveball. Handle the negative times with grace, maturity and patience. Say to yourself, slowly but surely, I will practice being positive even during difficult and trying times. Like any great athlete or musician, practice makes perfect, and yes, you can and should practice being perfect. One of Coach Paterno's sayings was, "Practice does NOT make perfect, perfect practice makes perfect."

Food for Thought

Suggestions to help you develop a positive attitude: the blog entitled, "Developing a Positive Lifestyle and Attitude".

1) *Listen to your internal dialogue.* Draw a line down a sheet of paper. For the next several days, write all your negative thoughts in the left column. Once you have several listed, rewrite each negative thought in a positive way into the second column. For example, *I need to lose 30 pounds* could become, *I will lose 5 pounds in one month through diet and exercise. I hate my job* becomes *I will start looking for a better job.* Things only

happen if you take a positive step toward making them happen.

2) *Communication is critical in developing a better attitude.* Although communicating your feelings can be difficult, it is necessary to learn how to do it. If you don't communicate, then you're inhibiting your growth.

3) *Stop focusing on yourself.* It will make you feel better about who you are. Helping an elderly person out or tutoring a child can really do a lot to make you feel better about yourself.

4) *Once you begin verbalizing your negative and positive thoughts, focus on your words.* For example, instead of command words such as, *no, don't, should* or *have,* use less judgemental words to express your needs, such as *I would appreciate it,* or *let's discuss how we.* Gracious language can express needs without judging.

5) *Find your sense of humor.* We can all take ourselves much too seriously. Laughter, humor and a quick wit are an excellent way to battle stress and calm your nerves.

LACK OF MOTIVATION TO CHANGE
(Why people don't pursue their passion)
Reason #7

"To improve is to change; to be perfect is to change often."
- Winston Churchill

The Fear of change is the trepidation you feel when leaving your comfort zone. You tell yourself that you're satisfied with what you have and where you are in life. You therefore will not explore opportunities or greater goals. I believe that we all owe it to ourselves to dream a larger dream and look for our higher calling. We only get one *dash* in life and it is our responsibility to fully embrace the passion in life.

In order for us to maximize our dash in life, we really need to understand what will motivate us to change and then take action. Research suggests that there are two motivating factors that cause people to change: pain and pleasure. The pain you feel may not be great enough for you to take action since the same experience might also give you pleasure. This if often the case with people in an abusive relationship or with a drug addict. Even though these situations are extremely toxic and painful, there are pleasurable at other times. You must be ready to break the status quo and truly want something better in life.

Staying the same is the easy way out

Doing things the same way doesn't require any thought. Staying in your comfort zone will assure you that you remain stagnant and reactive in life. As Albert Einstein said, "Insanity is doing the same thing over and over again and expecting different results."

> *"A dream is your creative vision for your life in the future.*
> *You must break out of your current comfort zone*
> *and become comfortable with the unfamiliar and the unknown."*
> *- Denis Waitley*

Over the years, I have experienced success and challenges as a professional, parent and partner. In accessing my challenges, I attribute many of the disappointments and setbacks to mostly being impatient and not thinking things through. As an example, my children have the ability to frustrate me on a wide array of topics, both significant and insignificant, relating to money, car pools, social situations and sleepovers. Typically, without really listening to what my children, my initial reaction to their demands had been to overreact and lecture them. Over the years, it became apparent that this wasn't working for either them or me. I was a painter using the same brush, same color, same canvas and expecting a more beautiful painting.

After standing back to look at my family portrait, I decided that I had to change my approach and step out of my comfort zone in order to change the picture. How was I going to create a new palette of warmer colors? Would my new approach help my relationship with my children or make it worse? How exactly would I change colors?

"Your life does not get better by chance,
it gets better by change."

– Jim Rohn

Changing my colors wasn't easy. It never is, if you think about it because there is that bleak fear factor associated with change. Fear is the color that can keep you locked in your cage painting the same picture day in and day out. I had been programmed for so many years. Ultimately, I realized that if I didn't change my parenting approach, my relationship with my kids would either remain the same or likely get worse.

When I sit back to look at my new family portrait, I can see that I have become a better father. Instead of imprudently reacting to my children's demands, I now listen to what their saying. In order for me to really listen, I need to be quiet and patient. I now talk to my children instead of talking at them. And if you find someone to help guide you in a positive direction, it's wonderful. My fiancee, Tina, has helped me with this process as she has provided support and direction in my growth as a parent.

LACK OF SELF-DISCIPLINE
(Why people don't pursue their passion)
Reason #8

"Mental toughness is many things and rather difficult to explain. Its qualities are sacrifice and self-denial. Most importantly, it is combined with a perfectly disciplined will that refuses to give in. It's a state of mind - you could call it character in action."

–Vince Lombardi

Self-discipline is diminishing in our modern culture as our friends, families and companies are losing to distractions and temptation. We have made an art of creative avoidance, indulgence, apathy and procrastination because we have been conditioned to believe that we deserve immediate satisfaction. Essentially, we've locked ourself in a cage because we have no long-term plan. Being self-disciplined is making the tough commitment change your life for the better.

Once you ask the question *how*, our creative juices and *can-do* mentality kicks in. Instead of dealing with the status quo, you need to ask yourself *how* you can obtain your passion in life. By doing this, you will force your mind and imagination to transcend limitations that will enable you to come alive. A subtle mind shift in your daily vocabulary can very quickly change your outcome. Suddenly, you will discover the powerful force growling within you, which makes you realize that you can take your game to the next level.

Success is just beyond the point when you feel like quitting. In your pursuit to be successful, it's important that you flip the switch to persevere and focus on your passion and goal.

Self-discipline is a learned behavior that gives you the ability to control your feelings and emotions. Self-discipline is one of the most important qualities to possess if you want to paint the life you really desire. Self-discipline is the capacity to overcome your perceived weakness and the ability to pursue what you want even when associates or your own insecurities try to derail you. Unfortunately, self-discipline is diminishing due to the distractions in our modern culture. Taking small steps will eventually lead to bigger and more successful ones.

*"Doing the easy things in life will make your life hard,
and doing the hard things first, will make your life easy."*

~ *Les Brown*

What does it take to be self-disciplined? If you have a passion in life or you are searching for that passion or purpose and you feel as if you have no self-discipline, I challenge you to think.

Think of something that creates fulfillment in your life. For instance, perhaps cooking or photography inspires you. Once you identify something that you love and do well, think about what it took to get to the level you are now. There was probably some preparation or learning involved. In order to become proficient at anything, there is practice, trial and error, and, finally, growth.

"The harder I play, the luckier I get."

-Gary Player

The impetus that kept you interested in developing that talent will be your foundation for self-discipline. It stands to reason that you will be more motivated and self-disciplined with a talent that is of great interest to you. The beginning process of implementing self-discipline in your life should begin with a talent or activity that drives your inner spirit.

If you think you should do something but you are not really interested in doing it, you won't be very successful with following through. Your desire is not really behind the action. You need to ascertain if your desire to implement self-discipline with a particular project is because you think you should, or because you really want to. Passion ignites momentum and inspires action. As my friend Ghaleb acknowledged, his profession as an architect was not his passion in life. His heart was empty. Fortunately, Ghaleb began the pursuit of his inner passion. He took the first step to open his cage. Today, he is a world renowned Latin American singer.

If your soul, emotions, physical energy, and intellect are not all in alignment with your passion, you are not fully vested in yourself. If you never follow through with what you perceive is your passion, then it could be that it is not your true passion or purpose. That's why the first steps of analysis and inner-dialogue are so crucial. It is important that you become clear about what it is that you really want. As the great Chinese philosopher Confucius said, "Choose a job you love and you will never work a day in your life." Following this simple, yet challenging endeavor will help you to take action on something that you will truly love and aspire to succeed at. Once you find it, anchor yourself in the joy of your inner passion.

It is equally important to learn what inspires and motivates you as well as learning what triggers negativity. You've looked at the bad, now take another step towards opening the cage door. Learn about who you are and what drives your inner spirit and passion. As we all know, it can be difficult to fight off urges and cravings, so it benefits you to know the areas where your resistance is low to avoid an urge. It is important to create an environment that is conducive and supportive of your ability to promote self-discipline rather than one that sabotages it. Reinforcement and pictures relating to your goals and aspirations are nice way to positively impact both your thought process and future actions. Change your palette to begin painting a more beautiful picture. Being able to visualize future achievements will help you develop a self-disciplined approach.

The Foundation of Self-Discipline

Self-discipline rests on the foundation of priority. What are the priorities in your life? Do you put yourself at the bottom of the list? Whenever you think of starting a new project to benefit yourself, do you tell yourself that you just don't have time! The reality of your situation is that you have many interests and obligations. Perhaps your list of daily activities is too long and should be trimmed down to a more manageable number that includes time for you.

> *"Discipline is the bridge between*
> *goals and accomplishments." – Jim Rohn*

LACK OF PASSION IN OUR CULTURE AND WORKFORCE

It is clearly evident that corporations throughout the world have not been successful in creating a passionate environment. From a financial point of view, corporations lose in excess of $200 billion a year due to the lack of workforce productivity. On average, the most productive employee wastes 1.5 hours per day on non-productive activity. Most recently, Gallup reported only 13 percent of employees worldwide are actively engaged in the workplace. That's the one who is emotionally involved in and committed to his or her work. According to Gallup's 2011-2012 study of employees in 142 countries worldwide, these findings represent a potent obstacle to job growth and economic recovery in many countries. Texting, lack of engagement, Facebook, gossiping and online shopping cost the average company $9,880 year per employee.

The typical employee wastes 25 percent of work time, or 520 hours per year. According to the U.S. Labor Department, there are about 116 million full-time employees in the United States. If the average employee earns $19 per hour while basically wasting 25 percent of their work day, then you can see how corporate financial earnings are affected negatively. One could hypothesize that the average employee is not happy or simply not engaged in any capacity at their job. Perhaps the majority of the workforce in the United States is not invested enough in their careers or jobs due to the fact that they are not living a purposeful life? By beginning the process of exploring passion and purpose, workforce productivity would increase.

In a global marketplace - where organizations have access to the same technology, communications and information - business leaders are grasping for answers. Yet the elusive competitive edge could be sitting right under their noses. Employers need to tap into and cultivate their employees emotional hot buttons so that they can produce at levels that will drive corporate profits and maintain employee morale. An engaged workforce that embodies the values and aspirations of the organization can transform an average business into a colossal success. But therein lies the challenge. How do business owners and managers drive motivation? How do leaders make their people passionate about their work when passion itself is so intangible?

There is a clear link between passionate staff members and productivity levels that employers need to capitalize on if they are to maximize financial performance while promoting the employees balance of life. In order for corporations to maximize financial gains, employers need to connect with individuals to provide them a purposeful, inspiration and motivational message.

In accessing the lack of passion in our corporations, one can hypothesize that top management and leadership has not embraced the idea of trying to establish a passionate work culture. Corporate leadership needs to establish and promote a culture of passion in the work environment. Identifying and implementing strong work values, honesty, job fulfillment and competence can be the first steps for top management to begin the journey. The extraordinary Apple Computer creator Steve Jobs was once asked what he could tell someone looking for career advice. His response: "Go out and get a job as a busboy or something until you find something you're really passionate about." CEO's and top management officials need to believe that motivation is linked to passion and this is the key to individual and team success.

A major cause of not achieving optimum corporate results can be attributed to the lack of passion in the workforce. With the strong and relentless demands of corporations throughout the world, it is easy to see how the employee has been lost in the shuffle of trying to maximize corporate earnings and shareholders profits. Slowly but surely, the tide is beginning to gradually shift back in favor of the individual employee. Management, human resources and corporate executives have made an assertive effort to better understand the employee's needs from both a personal and professional point of view.

Passion entails a number of factors; being in the right job is critical. Would an employee be better suited to another position within the company? Who are the employees that want to move up in the company? Is an honest effort being made to promote from within?. Working with the right team is a key factor to driving your motivation level. Creating a compelling corporate vision and establishing both its direction and focus is essential for team motivation and passion to be obtained. Finally, creating the right work environment facilitates passion, productivity and success for both the employee and organization.

Critically important to the success of cultivating a passionate work environment is hiring managers that understand the importance of passion in the workforce. Passionate leaders are the spark that foster commitment and determination among employees. Leaders who understand and embrace passion in their organization have tremendous opportunities for empowering their employees to meet desired goals. A passionate leader has the ability to create the kind of environment where their employees share their enthusiasm and drive to achieve organizational goals. In order to be an effective leader, you need to have passion for your work. This passion stems from believing that your work has significance and loving what you do.   Remember, passion breeds enthusiasm in others.

Passion can be encourage to create The Passionate Leader. This should be part of a personal mission for corporate leaders and top management. Leaders need to love what they do; otherwise, where are they leading their followers? If you lead with passion, your followers will learn from you.

You can grow your personal passion for your work. Reflection and introspection are great tools for growing your passion. Think about the following:

- *What makes you want to go to work?*
- *What energizes you at work?*
- *What keeps you going during a busy day?*

A passionate vision from top management without direction can be misguided to both middle management and the workforce. This can lead to the inability for the organization to understand priorities, focus and direction. No matter what goal or endeavor is the focus of your attention, there are proven strategies that can be implemented to help to transfer your passion to your employees. The goal is to move everyone in the same direction.

Create a Place Where Employees Want to Work

In a work atmosphere that promotes passion, inspiration and direction, absenteeism and turnover will decrease. Waking up in the morning and heading to a job that provides a culture of collaboration, communication and vision is exciting. You've unleashed a passionate crew. Morale and productivity will follow. Employee retention combined with enhanced financial performance and the ability to attract and to recruit top-notch employees will quickly ensue.

A passionate leader will breathe life into a lethargic work environment by promoting self-thought and thinking outside the box. More importantly, understand that it takes more than excitement to fully engage and motivate employees for the long haul. Organizational leaders and corporate top management know the key ingredients for a successful workplace includes employee involvement, communication and transparency.

Employees also want to work in places where their leaders are not only passionate, but communicate that passion every day in a myriad of ways. Whether it's face-to-face communication, a stimulating meeting, or a quick memo or e-mail, passionate leaders let their enthusiasm shine through. They also communicate the organization's triumphs and challenges to the employees before anyone else. Employees who feel trusted and involved come to share their leaders' passions and solidify their dedication to the organization.

Make Work Meaningful

One of the major reasons why we work is to earn a steady paycheck that provides us food, shelter and clothing. In addition to providing a paycheck, a passionate organization aims to offer a working climate that instills an all encompassing experience to employees, which harnesses both personal and professional objectives.

An organization that provides a culture of passion will exceed the expectations of its employees and shareholders. In order to help facilitate and drive a passionate organization, some companies appoint or hire a passion champion.

The role of the passion leader is to instill a sense of meaning and focus in their employees. A passion leader makes work more than just a paycheck. The passion champion could turn out to be a dissatisfied employee, who might be dissatisfied with the status quo. Mediocrity may not be an option for your restless employee who could be encouraged in passion and, in turn, raise the standards and performance of other employees.

The true passionate champion never wavers from the goal and will tolerate no less than the same passionate dedication from others. When distractions hinder employees and their performance, the passionate leader has the power to induce others to stay focused on the mission in hand. Passion is contagious and spreads throughout an organization, engaging and empowering employees along the way.

Leading with passion sends a clear message that permeates into every crevice of an organization. The bottom line is that passionate leaders need to spend time with their employees to understand what's meaningful to them. They will need to learn about their employees' wants and desires as well as how to communicate with their employees. Employees must feel the passion of their leader have more of their hearts and minds actively engaged in to put their heart into their work. Additionally, a passionate leader with an engaged workforce has a tremendous opportunity to create powerful change within an organization. With time, consistency and perseverance, passion will breed innovation and creativity into the culture of the organization.

If an existing corporation is not currently embracing a passion psychology into their overall vision, they should implement programs that will introduce passions into the workforce. In order to build passion, the Gallup Business Journal suggests:

1) Identifying the strengths of all employees so employees get the opportunity to do what they do best.

2) Measuring the extent to which people enjoy their work. Asses the individual passion level.

3) Understanding the motivating and demotivating aspects of the work environment.

4) Creating a compelling direction that is accepted and respected by the majority.

5) Instill meaning and purpose.

6) Create a sense of passion in your team.

7) Managing strategies to motivate staff.

8) Increasing motivating areas at work through organizations, and career development.

Once management incorporates a passion strategy into the culture, it is then imperative to maintain and monitor it. Paul Adofs *Eight Rules For Creating a Passionate Work Culture* includes:

Align all personnel to the newly formed culture: As with any change, existing employees might push back and fight change but please remember that it is critically important to transform and communicate the newly formed cultural mindset.

Hire the right people: Hire for passion and commitment first, experience second, and credentials third. It is important to find people who have the same expectations, goals and aspirations as you. This can be accomplished by asking the right questions: What do you love about your life and chosen career? What excites you about this career? How will you make a difference here?

Communication: Once you have the right people, you need to sit down on a regular basis to discuss problems and new ideas. A fertile culture is one that recognizes when things don't work and adjusts to rectify the problem. People need to feel safe and trusted to understand that they can speak freely without fear of repercussion. Remember that listening is as important as talking. Progressive cultures grow around people who listen to each other, to their clients and stakeholders.

Monitoring: An existing or evolving culture of passion can be compromised by the wrong people. One of the most destructive corporate weeds is the whiner. Whiners aren't necessarily public with their complaints. They don't stand up in meetings and articulate everything they think is wrong with the company. Instead, they move through the organization, speaking privately, sowing doubt, strangling passion. Sometimes this is simply the nature of the beast: they whined at their last job and will wine at the next. Sometimes these people simply aren't a good fit. Your passion isn't theirs. Constructive criticism is healthy, but relentless complaining is toxic. Identify these people and replace them.

Work hard, play hard: To obtain passion in a working environment, one requires a strong work ethic which can translate into long working hours. It's easy to do what you love. In the global economy, a superior work ethic can be measured in several ways. For instance, who is leading in productivity? Not many organizations or industries thrive on a 40-hour work week. A culture where everyone understands that long hours are sometimes required will work and sacrifice their personal interest for the benefit on the entire organization.

Be Ambitious: Ambition can be defined as a strong desire for success through hard work and determination. Ambitious people are always working towards a goal. People that have this quality are not the type of person to remain stagnate or sit still. Additionally, ambitious people will not only think about goals, they will take the initiative to pursue them. Ambitious individuals work through setbacks and adversity in the pursuit of their desired goals and aspirations.

Case Study No. 2

Pam Harris: Founder of Caring Voice Coalition

The Caring Voice Coalition (CVC) is dedicated to improving the lives of patients with chronic illnesses, accomplishing its mission by offering outreach services that provide financial, emotional and educational support. A very passionate and driven leader, Pam Harris started this wonderful organization from her home in 2003, initially employing only one person – herself. In the decade since, this national 501 (c)(3)non-profit has grown to employ a full-time staff of 50, with an annual funding budget of more than $85,000,000. Every year, the CVC helps thousands of people throughout the United States. Staff members understand that chronic disease deeply impacts a person's life. Doctors appointments, hospitalization and complex treatments make daily life hard to manage. Additionally, the financial and emotional strain can lead to fear, depression, and anxiety. The main objective of CVC is to empower patients to meet those challenges through programs and a knowledgeable, caring staff. The CVC values its reputation as a responsible, responsive organization with a unique, holistic approach to improving the lives of patients.

Over a three-month period, I had the honor of meeting Pam Harris to get a better understanding of why she chose this occupation. Pam acknowledged that, her passion at Caring Voice is also her passion in life. Getting up in the morning and going to work is definitely not a tough feat for Pam. Her desire to work and help people at CVC is her life's purpose. A typical 10-hour day seems like one hour in the eyes and mind of this compassionate leader. As I grew to know Pam, it became evident that this terrific lady is a selfless individual who gives more of herself then anyone I have ever met.

Raised in a large Christian family, with a strong, traditional moral and value system, Pam was taught at an early age to be emphatic and to serve others. At a critical time in her young adult life, her 21-year-old brother was tragically killed by a drunk driver, which greatly affected Pam as she struggled and grieved over the horrific event for many years. Through perseverance, grief, love and time, Pam was able to gather the strength and channel her brother's horrific death into a tool to provide strength to others. She was inspired to help others who faced arduous medical hardships and chronic illnesses. Over the years, Pam's passion and leadership have naturally evolved.

Training Your Mind

Over the last several pages, I have identified nine barriers that can prevent you from pursuing your passion in life. There are also specific strategies on how to work through these impediments so that you're able to get going in life by unleashing your purpose and passion. Making a conscious choice to change your behavior and apply specific action plans daily will help to drive your growth. Through a subtle mindset change and a well thought out implemented action plan you will begin to see a change in the way you think, act and behave. Please remember to stay the course and be patient as this process will take some time.

Since we have now grasped a thorough understanding of the barriers that impede us from pursuing our passion and purpose, it is now time to focus our time and attention on techniques that can be utilized in the pursuit of purpose and passion.

Next, you'll learn how to train your subconscious mind through conscious thoughts. Creativity, imagination and visionary thoughts will be the driving forces behind this next segment. Use these techniques to take your life to the next level. Before we begin this segment, I want to share the compelling story of Jean Lua as it relates to inspiration and passion.

Case Study No. 3
Jean Lua's dream come true

I was thoroughly impressed by the breadth and depth of work this young professional photographer was able to capture with her camera. Her work is rich in complexity, meaning and relevance. Jean's photographs truly sparked an emotional chord in me. As I looked at her art, I realized if she had ever had any chains binding her soul, they were broken. Here is a woman who must surely know her life's passion and purpose. I had to meet her.

I emailed Jean explaining the objective of my book. Within minutes, I received an email back from her. Her response was that of utter excitement and willingness to tell her story. Through our discussions, it became quite evident to me that Jean's purpose in life was being fulfilled by her passion for photography.

When I asked Jean how she feels when she snaps pictures, Jean clearly stated that she feels blissful, peaceful, directed and fulfilled. The camera lens is clearly a conduit that connects her eyes, heart and soul into one unified element, working in total synchronization.

As an Asian-American woman, Jean was raised in an affluent family in the Ohio area as the daughter of a prominent physician. She describes her upbringing as traditional and conservative, with values grounded in the importance of family, education, religion and hard work. For most of her adult life, Jean considered photography as nothing more than a hobby, although one that inspired her with awe as she snapped images of her world. But Jean certainly never dreamed about pursuing photography as a viable full time profession.

Following graduation from college with a degree in human resources, Jean pursued her career working with two organizations in the Northern Virginia area. For 13 years, Jean gained valuable career experience working in a team-oriented atmosphere with a positive company culture where growth and learning were emphasized. But something was still missing. Jean's inner passion and purpose had reverted back to her earlier days – back to her photography.

Through the teachings of God and her brother's strong words of encouragement, Jean decided to pursue her passion on a regular basis. She made a significant financial investment in professional camera equipment along with dedicating her time so she could adhere to a regimented educational schedule. She developed an insatiable appetite to learn about professional photography, which became the springboard she needed to take the leap of faith into her full time passion. With the eye of the tiger, Jean reached for her goal.

Energy, enthusiasm, passion and pure joy are the only words to describe Jean's feelings as she journeyed into her new career. In making the decision to pursue her passion in photography, Jean initially sacrificed a competitive salary, benefits and the peace of mind that comes with working in a well-established organization.

Following your heart, passion and purpose may impose a financial setback during the early years, but the long term fulfillment and satisfaction associated with following your dreams assures a deep sense of purpose and self-discovery. Every day, Jean has the privilege of waking up and getting out of bed to go to a job that provides her with the energy and excitement that we all want in our own lives.

CHAPTER 3

CREATIVITY AND IMAGINATION

Steve Jobs makes it sound easy. The Apple computers founder and CEO said, "Creativity is just connecting things. When you ask creative people how they did something, they feel a little guilty because they didn't really do it, they just saw something. It seemed obvious to them after a while. That's because they were able to connect experiences they've had and synthesize new things."

Apple is an innovative company that continually challenges the status quo. It has attracted classified misfits, rebels and pioneers. Apple computers has successfully led the technology charge to ignite mankind's most innovative and creative self. And they've made an enormous profit by doing so. Successful people utilize their creativity and imagination in ways other people don't. There's is a blank canvas waiting to be filled with vibrant, new colors. There's is a passion unleashed! Think outside the box to push your imagination and creativity in a new direction.

The imagination is the human workshop where ideas, concepts and creative thoughts are cultivated and refined. It has been said that man or woman can create anything he or she can imagine. People have discovered and harnessed more of Nature's forces during the last 50 years than during the entire history of the human race. Mankind's only limitation lies in the development and use of imagination.

How to incorporate imagination into your daily life

Ideas are the beginning points of all fortunes. They begin as the product of your imagination. Sometimes, the story starts on the day when a creator of ideas and a seller of ideas get together and work in harmony.

Andrew Carnegie surrounded himself with men who could do all that he could not do. Carnegie understood both his weaknesses and strengths. Through trial and error, he was successful in assembling an organization that blended great minds into a common goal that transcended the steel industry to make himself and others fabulously rich and successful.

Millions of people go through life in search of a favorable break or just plain luck. While a favorable break can foster opportunity, you shouldn't depend upon luck or coincidence. How great are your chances of actually winning the lottery? The safest plan is to generate your idea then implement it using determination, definiteness of purpose, and the desire to attain your goal. That's called hard work but it might not seem that way because you'll be working towards your own dream.

> *"We are all here for some special reason. Stop being a prisoner of your past. Become the architect of your future."*
> *– Robin Sharma*

Academician and world renowned expert on Innovation and Creativity, Sir Ken Robinson is a senior advisor to the J. Paul Getty Trust in Los Angeles. In 2003, he was knighted for his commitment to creativity and education. Sir Ken Robinson speaks about how human imagination and creativity in our public school system on a worldwide basis has been increasing neglected.

He points out that "creativity and imagination are a fundamental necessity when beginning the journey in identifying and exploring your passion and purpose. We're all born with immense natural and creative abilities that have been historically cultivated and nurtured through our educational system. It has become apparent that our youths and collegiate students have been robbed or limited in their creativity and imaginational strengths that have traditionally been offered through schools, universities and colleges. The international educational hierarchy has mandated stringent testing as well as standardization and academic compliance geared more towards Math, English and the Sciences. Unfortunately, by focusing on standardization and the culture of continuous testing, there has been a natural decline in the courses associated with the arts and the humanities, which has unequivocally damped the creative and imaginative sides of our academic and working population.

"Due to the reduction of the fine arts and humanities in the academic world, there has been a natural decline in our society to utilize one's imagination and creative capabilities ... If you are not able to actively imagine and utilize your creative sense, we can conclude that your ability to pursue a life of purpose and fulfillment can be somewhat more difficult since the utilization and implementation of your imagination is so key and critical to obtaining your passion" ...

"How can we rejuvenate and reinvigorate our imaginative nature to better tap into our passionate potential?"

You have been given the potential to develop a powerful, creative imagination to use for our benefit and possibly the benefit of all mankind. Everything mankind has achieved throughout its existence is a result of imagination.

Imagination gives you power! We all know about our other senses, hearing, sight, smell, taste and touch that signal our brain. These are defined as our animal senses. We need them to survive. Unlike other animals, the human brain evolved and took a quantum leap into an entirely new dimension. This new dimension would eventually open vast new secret worlds of nature to mankind. The developed brain allowed human beings to become creative and remarkably, gives you and I the unique opportunity to make decisions independently of our instinctive senses.

Throughout history, creative people have used their imagination to invent verbal languages, create powerful works of art, tell dramatic stories that touch hearts, develop customs that pass through generations, practice religion and eventually to write it all down. Human imagination has allowed mankind to climb from the valley of the ordinary to the peak of the mountains. Your imagination allows you to witness the marvels of nature, to paint pictures as no one has before you, to tell a story that has yet to be told. By unleashing your passion, you are changing the world.

In order to identify and cultivate your passion, you will need to increase your human potential by developing a powerful imagination. Just look around at the successful entrepreneurs, writers, artists, inventors, who have started new businesses, penned novels, songs and movies, invented new machines and other products. There is no limit to what you can achieve when your passion is unleashed. It's not easy, the prolific inventor Thomas Edison said, "Genius is 1 percent inspiration and 99-percent perspiration." If you are truly serious about your passion, having a powerful creative imagination at your disposal will help you identify and unleash your passion.

If you want to develop your creative imagination and find fulfillment in your purposeful life through a powerful creative imagination, you must open your mind to new paths, think of offbeat ways to tackle a problem and make something that is hard – easier. You have the potential to be creative, it is your special gift. Seize the opportunity to develop your unique gift and your horizon will fill with vibrant possibility.

Columbia Professor Donald Louis Hamilton offers some tips.

1)   *Be curious about everything.* The world is full of amazing wonders. They will become your storehouse of memories.

2) *Look deep into the problem you face.* Imagine a different alternative for solving the problem. Take new paths and don't accept the status quo. If you fail, try again. Try to visualize these problems as potential opportunities that can help you grow as an individual and human being.

3) *Develop your interests and natural talents.* Be curious and learn as much as you can about subjects you are interested in and then improvise, develop and expand them.

4) *Build upon the ideas of other people.* Improve and refine their ideas. This is a fundamental reason for human progress.

5) *Turn off the electronics and let your natural creative potential begin to kick in.* Being able to allocate a certain amount of stress free time allows maximum creativity to evolve. Exercise, taking a walk, dancing or perhaps gardening provides a soothing environment which promotes thought and creativity.

6) *Experience life.* Traveling and just living life are wonderful ways to promote creativity and imagination. There is no better way to broaden and refresh your outlook than traveling. It gets you out of an daily grind and exposes you to new people, customs and ideas. Traveling affords you the opportunity to view life in an entirely different light.

7) *Self-Reliance:* The more you depend on your own ability to think, the more proficient you will become at it. Experts and consultants should be viewed as collaborators and not individuals that are motivated and compensated to drive corporate decisions. In you rely on someone else to solve your problems and tell you what to do, your creative abilities will shrivel rather than flourish.

8) *Reading and Writing:* Reading and writing are considered to be a basic factor of creative aptitude. The act of writing forces you to utilize the creative process to form a tangible product.

CHAPTER 4

PERSEVERANCE AND GROWTH

*"Success is going from failure to failure
without losing your enthusiasm."*
                              – Winston Churchill

How do you keep moving forward toward your dreams and goals while roadblocks and obstacles seem insurmountable? Divorce, financial hardship and health issues may be among your personal struggles. Many days and nights, you might have had to justify your existence and purpose in life. Often, when you go through difficult times you develop patience, insight and wisdom. Realizing this can help lighten the blow. You might find yourself looking for the bad when good things happen. You just know it's coming. There's a giant pin on the horizon grinning evilly while it waits to burst your bubble. Why is it, then, that you fail to look for the good when bad things happen?

There are many inspiring, true stories of men and women who have beaten seemingly insurmountable odds and come out on top of the mountain. Yet not one of them was born with a sign around his or her neck that might have read, *Born for greatness*. Some inner drive propelled them to blaze a path of glory. With hard work, dedication and perseverance, you, too, are able to achieve astonishing success and stunning victories against seemingly insurmountable odds.

After more than 10,000 attempts at inventing the incandescent light bulb before he was successful, Thomas Alva Edison said, "Many of life's failures are people who did not realize how close they were to success when they gave up." Perseverance is steady persistence in a course of action, a purpose, especially in spite of difficulties or discouragement. Determination, tenacity and patience are closely related qualities. Play with the hand of cards that you're dealt.

"I learned that courage was not the absence of fear,
but the triumph over it. The brave man is not he who does
not feel afraid, but he who conquers that fear."
~Nelson Mandela

Not everyone is born into a royal family or blessed with wealthy parents. You can't control the external factors that may get in the way of your success. But what you can control is how you decide to deal with these obstacles. South African Civil Rights Leader Nelson Mandela changed the world for the better in spite of the fact that he was born into a society that deemed him a second class citizen. Like Mandela, you have struggles to overcome.

His lifelong goal, similar to Martin Luther King Jr., was to achieve equal rights for black people in his country. He was so dedicated to his cause that he spent a large portion of his life in prison for his beliefs and value system. While in prison, he became an inspirational leader and symbol for his people. After 27 years, he was released from prison and continued his fight for equality.

In 1993, Mandela won the Nobel Peace Prize for his efforts. His hard work paid off further when all South African citizens were allowed to vote in the 1994 election. Incredibly, Mandela became president of South Africa and to this day, is one of the most inspirational leaders and individuals that have walked this earth.

Walt Disney never let his failures stop him

As a young man, Walt Disney was fired from his local newspaper because his boss thought that he lacked creativity. He went on to form an animation company called Laugh-O-Gram Films in 1921. Walt was a great salesman and he was able to raise $15,000 for the company but, unfortunately, the New York distributor that he had partnered closed. When that happened, Laugh-O-Gram also had to close their doors. Barely able to pay his rent, Disney used his remaining money to buy a train ticket to Hollywood.

In Hollywood, Disney continued to persevere. Then, Mickey Mouse was born. Of course, the initial and now classical films were perceived by the studio and upper management as potential failures since they thought the mouse would terrify women. That never happened. Instead, Walt Disney became a magical name.

That wasn't the first time Hollywood moguls would be wrong. Distributors initially rejected *The Three Little Pigs* as well as *Pinocchio*. As you know, perseverance, determination and drive enabled Mr. Disney to succeed.

Disney's greatest example of perseverance occurred when Walt Disney tried to adapt the book *Mary Poppins* into a film. In 1944, at the suggestion of his daughter, Disney decided to adapt the Pamela Travers novel into a screenplay. However, Travers had absolutely no interest in selling *Mary Poppins* to Hollywood. To win her over, Disney visited Travers at her England home repeatedly over the next 16 years.

Overcome by Disney's charm and vision for the film, Travers finally gave him permission to bring *Mary Poppins* to the big screen. The result, of course, is a timeless classic.

Tough Times Will Become Better Times

> *"The ultimate measure of a man is not where he stands in moments of comfort and convenience, but where he stands at times of challenge and controversy."*
> *-Martin Luther King Jr.*

Whatever you current situation is, you must remember that it will not be permanent. Don't forget that your life will change. What's happening in your life and perhaps going wrong is a culmination of many events, beliefs and past actions. Your future can and will look very different if you are able and willing to make the conscious choice to change. You need to make the assertive choice to change the outcome of your life by understanding both the positives and negative behaviors that you have experienced in your life.

Begin to mentally prepare and visualize positive events and actions in your life through your thoughts, beliefs and actions. Creating and maintaining an aura of a positive mindset will help you to begin the process of directing your current life into a more positive, productive and enriched one.

Case Study No. 4

Meet an American Idol Golden Ticket winner

Singer/composer/guitarist Ghaleb is widely recognized as one of the most gifted, contemporary Pop/Tenor classical singers throughout the world. Ghaleb was born in Valencia, Venezuela, and by age 4, he began learning songs to entertain friends and family. As a somewhat shy 6 year old, he was named the winner of the El Festival del Nino (The Festival of the Child) celebrated on Mother's Day. Great things were on the horizon. By the time he was 12, Ghaleb began his studies at the Sebastian Echeverria Lozano School of Music and the Music Technology School of Valencia. He began performing to raise money for the reconstruction of several local hospitals.

In 2007, Ghaleb decided to compete in the seventh season of American Idol, a reality show with more than 140,000 performers and millions of viewers around the world. He stole the heart of the audience and went on to win the golden ticket to Hollywood, where he finished in the top 50. Ghaleb has a signature style of Latin influence with an Arabic flavor that people enjoy all over the globe.

I met Ghaleb when I was vacationing in Pompano Beach, Fla, in December 2013. Ghaleb was singing at a local club and as fate would have it, I had the pleasure and honor of hearing him perform. I was immediately enamored by the range of his voice and the notes he could reach with an elegance and grace that reminded me of a twinkling star way up in the sky. His sounds mesmerized an audience who flew with him on his celestial journey. Ghaleb's uplifting voice and soothing tone is proof positive he truly lives his passion. Following his performance, I introduced myself and we chatted about his music, message and sincere love for his art.

Ghaleb's is blessed with great talent and a true gift to connect with audiences. Despite his God given talent, his parental guidance as a young child and maturing adult was to pursue a career in Architectural design. His parents believed that performing would not provide a stable future for Ghaleb. The young man had to make a very difficult decision. Ghaleb realized that singing is his true passion and purpose in life. Ghaleb believes that living his passion and pursuing his dreams has provided him with a great sense of fulfillment, direction and meaning. Like Ghaleb, you owe it to yourself to unleash your passion.

What type of person are you?

For many reasons, there are people that don't want to look deep inside to tap into their natural calling. There are winners, losers and those who don't know how to win. Respectfully, I can only reach the individuals that have made the choice to explore and cultivate their inner passions. Equally, I expect to be able to help the people who do pursue a life of purpose and passion.

When it comes to unleashing passion, there are three types of people in the world. The first type of individual has the ability to connect with their inner passion or purpose. The second type of individual is simply not capable or chooses not to connect with their inner purpose. The third type is the person who wants to explore their purposeful side but has not been able to achieve it.

The first person has visionary capabilities to explore what purposeful meaning he or she possesses. This individual is not afraid to think outside the box and they are more than willing to begin the journey to find purpose and direction. Simply put, this person will do whatever it takes to achieve a life objective. Common traits include a vivid imagination and having a spiritual connection to a higher being.

As Coach Paterno told me on many occasions back in my college football days, was two distinct events happen on a daily basis.

"You either get better, or you get worse," Paterno said. "Unfortunately, there is no staying the same." Obviously, Coach Paterno was referring to football practice and how we needed to practice and to give 100 percent each and every day.

If you think about it, footballs a lot like life that also changes every day. You need to prepare for life, too. As our sage coach was providing us words of wisdom relating to football, he was in his masterful way preparing us for life.

As football players initially and later on, we all had a choice to either make ourselves better each and every day. We can also choose to remain stagnant. Coach Paterno inspired me to live these words of wisdom on a regular basis.

Conversely, the second person is not able, or does not desire, to pursue their intended life purpose. Perhaps they are stagnant in their life and have made the chosen to be content with where they are in life. Procrastination, the devils will, can defray your ability to grow and promotes the stifling of your individual pursuit for purpose and fulfillment. Excuses, complicity and resting on your laurels are equally responsible for hindering growth and purpose.

The third person is the one individual that has the ability and desire to obtain purpose but can't take it to the next level. Fear, frustration, lack of time, little to no direction can all be reasons why someone is unable to identify purpose. With some coaching, these people are able to fulfill their life's passion.

CHAPTER 5

HOW TO BEGIN TO IDENTIFY YOUR PASSION?

"I would rather die of passion than of boredom."

– Vincent van Gogh

We have identified the major barriers that typically impede you from pursuing your passion and purpose in life. By looking at the world around you differently, you can now embark on the exciting journey of taking your life to the next level. Congratulations, you are standing at the door, ready and willing to be unleashed!

A fundamental step in finding your passion is to live a healthy lifestyle both mentally and physically. Unleashing your passion will require a strong mental awareness that can be obtained by eating right, exercising reasonably and living a clean lifestyle. Identifying and pursuing your passion is an individual choice and one you have obviously made. Bravo.

New Age Author Shakti Gawain offers suggestions to find your passion. "When you're following your energy and doing what you want all the time, the distinction between work and play dissolves."

As wonderful as this sounds, it can be difficult to figure out what you love and then turn it into a viable business or job. Remember, a passion doesn't necessarily have to be a full time occupation or career, it can also be a weekend or part time hobby that provides meaning, direction and purpose in your life. I have put together a step-by-step plan for zeroing in on your passions and how you can begin the process of making these aspirations part of your life.

Identifying and Taking Hold of Your Passion

1) Remembering What You Loved as a Child. Being the lead drummer in my grade school Jazz band was a wonderful time in my life. Playing a broad range of songs and beats, ranging *In the Mood* by Glenn Miller to the legendary 1968 drum solo of *In-A-Gadda-Da-Vida* by Iron Butterfly, were times in my life that I look back on endearly way. Many passions are cultivated in childhood, only to be overtaken later on by real life pressures. Remember what you loved long before you had to worry about your career? Baking? Art? Writing? Cooking? Getting back in touch with those instincts is an important step in finding your passion.

2) Eliminate Money from the Equation: If money were no object, what would you do? Would you travel to spend time on an exotic island, spend all your time with your children? Perhaps you would start a charitable organization to help motivate teenagers? Of course, money can't be ignored but don't let financial pressures dictate your choices. Your career should lead to financial security, but if financial security is the defining motivator, it's unlikely you'll end up doing what you love.

Don't Be Afraid to Ask

You're not always the best judge of what makes you happy. Talk to friends, family and co-workers. Ask for them when they think you are the most happy. Ask your friends what are you good at? Their answers may surprise you, as well as to help guide you in a new direction.

Role Models Are Important

Having a strong parental figure as a youngster is critically important to development. It is equally important to have someone that you would like to emulate and be like as an adult.

Of everyone that you know or know of, whose career would you most want to emulate? If you identify someone, take the next step and research everything you can about that person and their career path. Utilize the internet and other social venues to connect and learn about topics and people that inspire you.

Create a Dream List

Focus on the things that you both enjoy and do well – whether you have a knack with helping people, seem to have been born with a spatula in your hand, or are passionate about helping neglected animals. Then, narrow the list to the top three or four things and put them on your Dream List. Keep this Dream list handy to review often. Revise and update this list to use as your when you're planning a career move.

Giving Back: The Higher Calling

We all have a higher calling in life and it's your responsibility to pursue your passion since you will be affecting humanity in a positive way. When you unleash your passion, you function at your peak performance because your heart, mind and soul are invested fully in this pursuit. This will transcend those that you touch and, in turn, affect them in a positive light.

Growing up in the suburban Philadelphia area, my father was my inspiration, coach and mentor. He was a high school and college professor teaching chemistry, math and physics. I never had the opportunity to be in my Dad's class but it was apparent that my father had motivated many of his students to excel. Dad was obviously living his passion as a teacher. Teaching was the fuel that energized my father's passion.

Throughout the years, I had the privilege of meeting many of my father's former students. They would often start to tear up. I could feel the warmth of their admiration for my Dad.

One student, now a nurse, said "Your father was the most inspirational and guiding person in my life. Not only was he a terrific teacher that educated us and made us laugh, he also had a wonderful way of making us all feel special." She continued by saying that my father not only helped her to get into West Chester University's School of Nursing, but he was also successful in helping her secure her financial aid and grants, which basically paid for her entire college. I cherish this story and so many more about my Dad.

My dad was very fortunate in life to find his passion and to have a wonderful career as a teacher and life coach. Like my Dad, when you are living your passion in life and finding a greater purpose, direction and meaning, you will also be giving back to humanity in some way. You will then be living and pursuing your higher calling in life. To me, this is the epitome of what your life should represent.

Getting Started

Once you begin identifying your passion, it's time to take action to begin the process of unleashing it. Some good steps that you might want to take are:

Talk to a Career Counselor or Life Coach

1) Career counselors and life coaches offer guidance about what you want to do for a living. They provide insight and the tools to help you zero in on the things you love most and do best.

2) *Leverage Social Media.* More than ever, we live in a connected world. Once you have identified what it is that you love, get busy and explore Facebook, Twitter and LinkedIn. You'll be surprised by how many people will support you in pursuing your passion.

3) *Start Saving Money.* Once you feel strongly that you want to start down this new path, get out your piggy bank. The more you save, the more relaxed you'll feel, which will provide you peace of mind.

4) *Just Do It.* Stop procrastinating. You won't really know what you love to do unless you actually bite the bullet. Until then, it's really just speculation - a pipe dream. Whether you test the water by learning more about your passion or dive in head-first, you'll never unleash it until you try. Best of luck to you and please continue striving to find purpose and make your life more fulfilled. Go ahead. Unleash your passion.

CASE STUDY NO. 5

Steve Smith: A story of purpose and meaning

I have had the honor and privilege of knowing Steve Smith for the past 30 years. Steve and I met as football recruits at Penn State University back in the early 1980s. Steve was an intimidating 6-feet-2-inch, 240 pound Parade All-American fullback from the highly touted DeMatha Catholic High School in Hyattsville, Maryland. Every major college and university throughout the county solicited him for both his athletic and academic capabilities. Steve selected Joe Paterno's nationally ranked football program for many reasons.

During our five years at Penn State together, Steve and I became good friends both on and off the field. Whether we were scrimmaging during the scorching August heat in Happy Valley, playing pranks, partying or studying at our mandatory study halls, Steve and I formed a lifelong friendship. Following graduation from Penn State and earning two National Championships, Steve and I traveled different paths in life as he was drafted in the 3rd round to the Los Angeles Raiders while I pursued a professional career in corporate America and began graduate school. Steve and I lost contact due to the demands and obligations of our lives.

In 1990, as luck would have it, I was transferred out to beautiful Southern California where I lived as a young bachelor. Steve on the other hand, had several years under his belt as a professional football player and had married a terrific young lady named Chie, a former Raiderette and California resident. Together, Steve and Chie were blessed with two beautiful children, Dante and Jazmin.

After settling into my new life, I reached out to Steve. We agreed to meet at his house. I was excited to see my college buddy and to meet his new family. Following the hour and half drive into Orange County on the infamous 405 freeway, I arrived at Steve's house in Redondo Beach. I met Chie and Steve's wonderful children. After, Steve and I reminisced about our Penn State day and discussed our current lives. Even though our lives at that moment were very different, we still shared the common thread of friendship and history.

Over the next several years, Steve and I would visit until destiny once again separated our paths. I got an exciting job opportunity back in the Philadelphia *and following Steve's professional football career, Steve and his family moved to Texas.*

Back in Philly, my life moved quickly. I started a new family and, as I am sure that you can imagine, the demands of career and family made it difficult to maintain communication with Steve on a regular basis.

Since life was good on my end, I assumed that all was well with Steve and his family. In recognition of the national championship football teams from 1982 and 1986, the university planned events to honor them. Steve and I both attended with our families. We would golf on Friday then attend a dinner with former teammates and their families. The festivities would continue into football Saturday with pre-game tailgates, autograph signing, and rekindling with teammates, coaches and managers.

When we walked out onto the field at halftime to be singularly recognized, the cheers carried me back to the glory days. Over the 20 years of reunions it was great sharing the turf with Steve once more. We reveled in the thousands of fans who came to show their appreciation. We are ... Penn State.

As in years past, I expected to see my good buddy Steve bouncing into the 25th reunion. I had never bothered calling him. It was a given he'd show. Right? When
Steve's father and two children walked in the door, I felt relieved as I looked behind them for Steve. But Steve didn't follow.

Steve had been diagnosed with ALS-(Amyotrophic lateral sclerosis), better known as Lou Gehrig's Disease. He'd had it for years and I never knew. Steve and his family had kept the tragic news to themselves.

I couldn't help but feel guilty that somehow I had let my friend down. I felt guilty that I had not stayed closer to Steve. After talking with Steve's wife Chie, I learned that the only way to communicate with him was through a state of the art computer system.

The blinking of Steve's eyes would activate and transcribe his blinks into words. The ALS disease had progressed rapidly and immobilized Steve to his living room hospital bed. I began emailing Steve and sending pictures that carried us both back
to the days when responsibility was just a word in the dictionary and football, study and Penn State frat parties filled our lives.

As I began writing this book, it became clear to me that Steve and his life would be a wonderful addition due to his extraordinary circumstances and his brave journey in battling this serious disease. Steve's story is a true example of someone who is living their purpose in life, despite his state of health. As a former professional athlete and lead blocker for NFL Hall of Famer Marcus Allen and All-Pro running back Bo Jackson, Steve played the game of football with great passion, purpose and determination. Steve's pregame talks helped inspire us to victory. His passion and leadership on the field led us to glory.

As a father, husband and son, Steve Smith is passionate in these roles and dedicated to being the best man he can be. Today, Steve's life purpose has expanded to being an inspirational and brave role model despite his debilitating ailment. The meaningful journey that Steve is currently embarking upon is providing strength and motivation to others who witness his daily battle in fighting the ALS disease.

It is interesting to evaluate the decisions you have made that have created the "dash" in your life. The purpose or passion that you elect to pursue are of your own free will and volition. Steve has bravely embraced this new purpose for the benefit and well being of others. I can assure you that my good friend Steve Smith has made the mental decision to look at his life as the glass as half full. Being thankful for what you have and pursuing your life purpose with enthusiasm, vigor and excitement is the key to living a fulfilled and meaningful life. It is the key that you will use to open the cage door and unleash your passion.

(At top) **Penn State** players are led onto the Beaver Stadium field by legendary Coach Joe Paterno. (Bottom L to R): **#33 Steve Smith-3rd Round Draft pick**, #42, D.J. Dozier-All-American, and #25 Game Captain Drew Bycoskie discuss strategy.

Pennsylvania's Top Teacher: My dad, John Bycoskie has guided and inspired his students, while continually learning and having fun for over three decades. Dad has always been my #1 fan and has always supported me in all my endeavors. Thanks dad.

Pam Harris and CVC is dedicated to improving the lives of patients with chronic illnesses.

Ghaleb, World renowned Pop/Tenor Classical singer is living his singing passion. Ghaleb, American Idol Finalist entertains fans throughout the world.

At the Penn State game with great friends and former teammates Dean DiMidio and David Clark.

Gary Guller-World Recorder holder Mt. Everest Summiteer inspires individuals and organizations to pursue their individual potential.

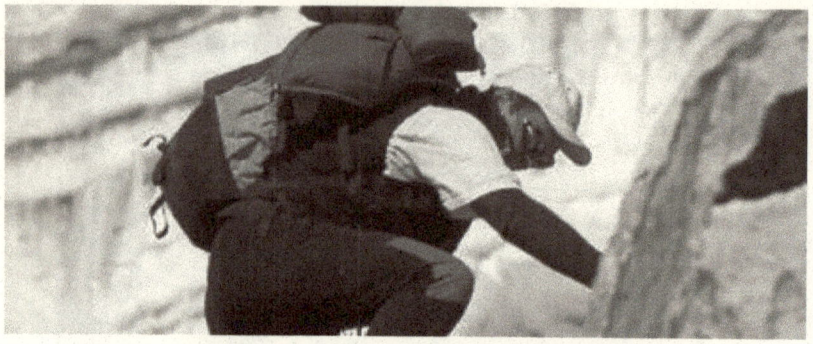

Dad with my sister Pam and my three beautiful daughters, Elly, Chloe and Bergen.

Modern Family:
Celebrating a festive Christmas with Jake in the middle of five
beautiful ladies. Kate, Bergen, Chloe, Elly and Lauren.

Graduation day at the Air Force Academy. (L to R. Harry, me, Max and Tayler)
Three terrific young men.

Enjoying a terrific dinner, courtesy of my brother in law, Michael (L to R) Michael, nephew Tayler and sister Pam. (Front) Elly, Bergen & Chloe

Best of Times: Mom & Dad with Harry and Max

My fiancé Tina has inspired and encouraged me to pursue my Passion in life.

CHAPTER 6

MENTAL VISUALIZATION

Now that you have begun the process of identifying your passion, the next step is to visualize your future purpose and passion. A prerequisite in pursuing your passion is to imagine where you want to be and how you want to get there.

"The person you see is the person you will be. Your mental images are your previews of your life's coming attractions."

-Jim Cathcart

As Albert Einstein said, "Imagination is more important than knowledge." Knowledge is limited, Einstein continued. Imagination, on the other hand, stimulates progress. By utilizing your imagination, you are mentally preparing yourself for the exciting journey that you have embarked upon. An important part of visualization is to feel yourself performing the way you want. Be strong, confident and focused. Many athletes and professionals use imagery as a technique to build confidence and prepare for a game or a business meeting. Imagery can also be used to plan strategies, rehearse game plans, or as a way to cope under pressure. Everyone has the ability to use imagery. Like anything else, it is a skill that must be developed through practice.

How does imagery and visualization work?

First, research has demonstrated that imagery strengthens the neural pathways for certain movements. A neural pathway is like a superhighway of nerve cells that transmit messages and information from one part of the brain to the other. When you exercise the neural pathways, you can imagine yourself performing a particular sport or cognitive skill, which, in turn, activates your muscles and brain neurons to operate as if you are actually performing the task. Secondly, imagery may function as a coding system in the brain to help athletes and others form a plan or mental blueprint enabling their actions to become perfunctory.

Back in the old days, in addition to being a strong safety at Penn State, I was also a place kicker for Joepa. As any kicker will tell you, mental preparation is a key component associated with kicking a football in front of 64,000 thousand football fans. Before you kick, you have to visualize the hike of the football, holding it, for a split second you close your eyes and see it soaring between the poles, like a knight easing by the castle guards.

It takes both physical and mental practice to master any art, whether it's a sport or a cognitive act like dealing with an ornery child or dysfunctional relationship, it takes preparation and practice to deal with it effectively. You will develop a subconscious awareness of how and what you want to accomplish. And then, you will succeed.

Recent research has focused on the effectiveness of imagery as an important self-regulated skill set (i.e., the ability to set goals, plan and solve problems, as well as to control and regulate anxiety and effectively manage other emotions.) The key is to program your mind, muscles, and emotions for success and to make your mental imagery as vivid, realistic and detailed as possible. When you imagine yourself embarking upon the journey to unleash your passion or identify what your purpose in life is, your central nervous system will become programmed for success as if the activity you visualize has already happened.

Visualization and mental rehearsal does work. The best part is that you can do it anytime and anywhere. The subconscious mind cannot tell the difference between fantasy and reality so really dig deep to picture your goal.

The first step that I recommend to visualize a goal is to write it down. Use a pencil since you might want to modify it in the future. One of my goals that I wrote was to *become a better, more tolerant and understanding father* (easier said than done). By writing your goal down, you are committing to something tangible since you will be able to reference the document, thereby holding yourself accountable.

In other words, by simply experiencing the emotion of having your passion fulfilled, the reality of those feelings become real to you through the Law of Attraction. You need to visualize the success of your passion by seeing it and feeling it. Focus on your game. See your goal. Unleash your passion.

Be intense and dream vividly

Vividness – a vivid image is intense. The key is to use as many senses as possible - see the action, feel yourself moving, hear the sounds and smell the smells. Be as detailed as possible when you paint the picture in your mind. Know what it feels like as if it is actually happening. For instance, Sport Psychologist Kick Coop suggests golfers incorporate two levels of visualization on every shot:

1) Create a mental movie on the way you want the ball to fly.

2) Translate that picture into a realistic imagine of how the body should move in order to hit the shot. Feel the rhythm. As with kicking a ball, swinging a golf club or imagining a passion, create the most intensely detailed image so that you can accelerate the physical law of attraction.

> *"It doesn't matter where you are, you are*
> *nowhere compared to where you can go."*
> *– Bob Proctor*

Here's how to use mental imagery to be a stronger and more focused person. As we have discussed, mental imagery has long been employed by professional athletes and business professionals to boost their strength, confidence and results. Wayne Gretzky, arguably the greatest ice hockey player ever, has always used mental visual techniques to improve his performance on the ice. One of Wayne's most famous quotes is that "he would skate to where he thought the ice hockey puck was going to be in relation to where it actually was at that specific moment." For Wayne, anticipating and visualizing in the sport of hockey helped make him a success.

Sports aside, these same techniques can be instilled in every arena of your life. Research has shown time and time again that surgeons, musicians, and business executives have used mental visualization to help focus and to improve their performance. I used it in my personal life to help me be a better dad.

It's imperative to mentally visualize your passion several times a day. It would be my recommendation to visualize your passion at least three times a day for at least five minutes at a time. Perhaps before you go to bed at night, take some quiet time to visualize your passion. Suppose for a moment that you were a chef. You might visualize the process of cooking a special meal, marinating the chicken with oil and lemon, then seasoning it with thyme, salt and pepper. Know your goal, then determine the times you'll set aside to visualize. Remember, you've embarked on this journey. Don't let finding the time become a roadblock to your success. Practice your breathing when visualizing your goal - slow and steady breaths.

The repetitive actions of mental visualization will help to drive and fulfill your passion by stimulating your brain neurons. In addition to the visualizing of your passion, you are concurrently working with a series of predetermined action plans that will help to launch your passionate focus into play.

CHAPTER 7

LET'S GET THIS SHOW ON THE ROAD

Getting in touch with Your Core Beliefs

Your personal power and the ability to attract what you want will be strongest when what you want to happen is exactly what you expect to happen. Believing that you can obtain your passion in life is an essential component of your success. Your beliefs are the foundation upon which all your expectations are formed. According to the Law of Attraction, they are the energy magnets that pull in what you think is true about yourself and the world around you.

It's part of God's plan and the Law of Nature that life doesn't feel right when your core beliefs do not agree with who you really are. The feeling of being disconnected is the cause of all negative emotions. In our heart of hearts, we can sense when we are not following our core beliefs.

"Change your thoughts and you change the world."
-Norman Vincent Peale

As an example, my family upbringing was that of a loving and caring environment in which both my mother and father were very involved in all aspects of my life. Mom and Dad were always available to me. Very simply, one of my core beliefs that was developed and nurtured over the years was to be a loving and caring father and parent to my future family.

Once I had become a father of three beautiful daughters, I was a supportive and caring father who took an active and caring role in their lives. Yes, there were times when I might have lost my temper or yelled like a lunatic at them but overall, my children received love and attention from me through their early years. Unfortunately, when my children were young teenagers, I had gone through a divorce and during this time in my life, I was not a quality father like I had been before. My availability to love, provide guidance and just to be with my children had diminished since my life was turned upside down. I was not following one of my core beliefs and values relating to being a good father and I felt a sense of disconnection with God and disappointment in myself.

Thankfully, I was able to get back the core belief that I was raised with and able to re-establish myself as a loving, caring and very involved father to my children. The quality of your life is a direct result of the quality of your beliefs. On the physical level, your core beliefs cause you to think and behave in a specific way that either support or suppress your personal power. They are rooted in your subconscious mind and in theory, you don't need any type of psychoanalysis or in-depth study to identify and change them.

Your beliefs are simply the thoughts you keep thinking until they describe your reality. You can easily change your conscious beliefs when new information presents itself. When you were a child, you established your unique core beliefs. As you moved into your teen years, despite how entrenched your core beliefs might have been, we still potentially could change your beliefs in a relatively simply fashion. Obviously, you have to first identify what your core beliefs are and to accomplish this, all you have to do it is pay attention to your *I am's*. Your I Am's will point directly to your core beliefs. What goes on in your subconscious is revealed moment by moment in your conscious mind by what you attach your *I am's* to. Your attachments either align with or resist your true nature.

When you think *I am* tired of being poor, arguing, being overweight, drinking too much or doubting who you are, realize that you have a strong attachment to not having what you want. By having this mindset, you are claiming it for yourself every time you entertain that thought. When you think that *I am* not ever going to be financially free or *I am* never going to be in a wonderful relationship, you are claiming that thought as your reality. Eventually, these thoughts become your core beliefs and, hence, your reality.

When you feel sorry for yourself and have an internal dialogue like, *"I'm tired of not being more financially successful"* or *I am tired of being poor,"* you are creating a life based on your core belief that you don't deserve an easier, more abundant life. For you, life is about struggling and not having enough to support your lifestyle. You are resisting who you really are.

One of my daughter's attends the local high school. She is smart, beautiful, friendly, hard-working and an aspiring young lady. At times though, she is very negative in her thoughts and perceptions of both herself and of life in general.

Once, when I was picking her up from work, the first words out of her mouth where negative comments and condescending remarks relating to her self-worth, work, friends and school. As she sat slouched in the car seat with a frown on her face, she made the concerning statement that "I am not a happy person and I am ugly. Nobody likes me and I never have any money. Life stinks." She was so distraught, she broke down and cried.

I offered to take her to Wawa, a beloved local convenience store, to distract her. Surprisingly, she declined my offer and we continued to drive in the now silent car. After a time, I began, "Your negative feelings, thoughts and words only attract negative results in your life. You need to select your words and thoughts more carefully and simply be more positive."

I told her what a terrific young lady she is. "Look at what God has blessed you with and utilize that as your thought process foundation," I said. My speech concluded by asking her to sit up in the car seat, get a smile on her beautiful face and look deeply into to her heart think about the wonderful talents and blessings that she has.

With my daughter's situation and for other people looking to move forward, you need to begin the process of changing your core beliefs, which serve as self-imposed barricades to your passion. You need to attract what you want in life by understanding and attracting what objective, passion or purpose that you desire. This is mandatory if you want to unleash your passion.

In order to move past these limiting beliefs and barriers and to take your life to the next level, you need to catch yourself in the act of *I Am-ing* and consciously choose to think something that evokes a more positive emotion. The power of thought and positive beliefs are what change your core beliefs, which ultimately will lead you to identify and pursue your passion.

From every moment moving forward that you are not happy with your life, it presents an opportunity to transform your negative core beliefs into a positive and life changing belief. For example, my daughter needs to dig deep and pull out positive beliefs.

In order to do this, she will have to change negative behaviors and her Debbie-downer attitude. She needs to look at her life in a different way and appreciate what she has. As an example, relating to issues with her money situation and her job, my daughter's inner dialogue should sound something like "I appreciate that I have a job at the store even though I don't make the money that I really need. Since I have started at the store, I have been promoted into a Team Leadership position and I will continue to seek additional opportunities from to see how I can increase my earnings."

With a simple shift in your inner dialogue, you can quickly start on the road to attracting positive thoughts, beliefs and more importantly, positive results. The more you imagine with a grateful and open mind what that perfect life looks like and how it feels to have it, the more you will be able to release your old *I am* attachment to struggle and suffering. The more you expect to receive what you want in life, the faster it falls into place. We resist remembering who we really are because we can. We have free will and the freedom to turn toward or away from accepting our true nature and to unleash our passion.

Your conscious or rational mind has many jobs. It interacts with the world, interprets your five senses, solves problems, and most importantly, follows the direction of your core beliefs. Recently, I learned a valuable technique that has helped me to keep at bay the occasional recurring limiting *I am* thoughts. When you catch yourself entertaining a limiting *I am* thought about a subject such as taking a financial or emotional risk, and as quickly as possible say to yourself, *"Thank you for sharing. What I really believe is.* (fill in the blank with a positive declaration of what you want and deserve to be, do, or have)."

This simple technique works so well because thanking yourself disarms your perception of danger (moving outside your comfort zone) and helps you to replace the self-limiting belief with a new belief that supports your desire. It enables you to remember who *I really am*. This may seem strange but try to position your mind as a friend who wants to supports your beliefs, hopes and aspirations. You are your best friend and most supportive self.

Limiting core beliefs can be hidden in the *I Am* that will take various forms such as *I have* or *I hate*. For example, an *I can't* example is *I can't do that* or *I don't know how."*

If you pay attention to what you were thinking when you started feeling bad, and choose thoughts that shift your energy toward the future you want to have, you are moving in the right direction.

You know you are making progress when *I can't do that* becomes *Thank you for sharing. What I really believe is that I can do that when I'm ready, and I'm getting more prepared to do that every day.*

My upbringing won't let me be in a good relationship since my parents divorced becomes *thank you for sharing, what I really believe is that even though my parents divorced, my parents had a good relationship for many years and I will build on that aspect of my parents relationship in my own relationships.* As you can see, by subtly changing your inner dialogue, your belief system begins to change.

You can enhance your progress by writing down your limiting *I Am* as they creep into conversations or your thoughts. up. Later, when you have some quiet time, write down the answers that will help you move past your limiting belief.

The key is to make the choice to stop lamenting about your current situation and think about what you want in life. Once you make these positive choices and begin to visualize what you really want, you are crossing a threshold to finding your true core beliefs. You may have to step over that threshold a hundred times, but if you keep doing it, one day you'll notice that the threshold is behind you and things are really looking up! The rest is a matter of keeping your momentum going and never sliding back into your old *I Am.*

You must keep making conscious choices to imagine a new *I Am* until the limiting ones stop surfacing. You may need to forgive yourself to leave some old *I Am* baggage behind. In time, you will be too busy choosing between opportunities and new positive thoughts to regress into those old, self-defeating habits. As long as you are committed to being the conscious creator of your own life, your visionary mindset and new thought process will prevail.

The Law of Attraction is Absolute

Like attracts like, focus causes expansion, and the universe offers limitless possibilities. Letting go of negative thoughts helps you go where you want to go at warp speed. It will also raise your perspective to a higher level allowing you to take more powerful and life affirming actions.

If you will do this consistently, you will exponentially increase your power. Your life will change drastically because you have empowered yourself. You will no longer be painting a dull picture. Open the cage door to take your rightful place among the conscious creators who choose happier thoughts and a more fulfilled, passionate life.

Summary

You have embarked on a commendable and exciting journey towards growth, inner strength and a more fulfilled life. Remember, it's not going to be easy but with due diligence, you will unleash your passion. Unleashing your passion is truly finding your personal road map to a purposeful and meaningful life. Obtaining this wonderful gift requires determination, perseverance and a strong mind set to change your thoughts, actions and beliefs. Many things will work against you. They often include limiting beliefs, fear of success, procrastination, associating with the wrong crowd, attitude, lack of motivation to change and lack of self-discipline. There is also a lack of passion in our culture and workforce that could be holding you back. Understanding what the Limiting Barriers are that keep you detached from your life passion. You must change your behavior. Take proactive steps to understand and to ultimately conquer these limiting barriers.

You will lead a more passionate and purposeful life. You can and will do this. The door will open and a confident, intense you will emerge victorious in the knowledge that you have painted a new and magnificent picture for your life, rich in color and texture. It is the fabric of change and you are the eye of the tiger. You are your own champion!

Six Steps to Successfully Unleash Your Passion

As you have learned, utilizing a visualization and creative thought strategy will help accelerate your ability to identifying and pursue your passion. The remaining step to unleash your passion is to implement an action plan to stay focused on your purpose.

Step One

Imagination-Dream: What do you really want in life? Identify where you want to be one or two years from now. The imagination is literally the workshop to develop an idea into a reality. Take the leap of faith and really dig deep to identify what you desire most. Once you find a passion that you truly love, whether it's a hobby, a career, or a new lease on life, you will be fulfilled.

Pick up a pen or pencil to write down three passions that you want to obtain within a year time. Keep your paper close so that you can visualize your future goals. You are holding yourself accountable.

1)_____

2)_____

3)_____

Step Two

Positive Mental Visualization: The mental images you create are the previews of your life's coming attractions. By visualizing it, you are mentally preparing yourself for the exciting journey. Before you go to bed, visualize where you want to be one year from now. Perhaps you want to be in a strong relationship or perhaps you want to be in a more stable financial situation or perhaps you want to start a charity.

You are the artist that paints the picture of your life. Positive thoughts, sincere emotions and a strong belief system will help summon what you want though the energy of our interconnected universe. If you truly want to paint a vibrant painting, you only need to think differently and believe it. The quality of your life is a direct result of the quality of your beliefs and thoughts. These are the keys to the cage door.

Write the specific times that you plan to visualize your future promises or passions! I would suggest 15 to 30 minutes per day, once in the morning, afternoon and then again before bed. Also, please write what exactly you will be visualizing.

1)_____

2)_____

3)_____

Step Three

Changing Your Beliefs: Your personal power, the ability to attract what you want, is strongest when what you want to happen is what you expect to happen. Believing that you can obtain your passion in life is necessary for success. Your core beliefs are the foundation upon which all your expectations are formed. They are the energy magnets that pull toward you – via the Law of Attraction - what you think is true about yourself and the world around you.

Moving forward, from every moment in which you aren't happy about your life, make the mental commitment to look at this situation as an opportunity to transform your negative (resisting) core beliefs into positive and life changing beliefs. Looking at the glass as half full in comparison to the glass as half empty is a good start. If you are experiencing financial difficulties, relationship issues or depression, take a good hard look at these setbacks and see them as opportunities to grow as a human being. You will emerge stronger of you take the right steps now. The more you can imagine you perfect life, the more likely you are to unleashing your passion and purpose.

Step Four

Subtle Mind Shift: Looking at Life: Instead of looking at challenges in life as issues and problems, you need to refocus and look at these situations as personal growth opportunities. For whatever reason, you were derailed in pursuing your passion. You owe it to yourself to get back on track.

Please identify three issues or problems that you are facing in your life that you can change into opportunities. (i.e., I have not been able to have a stable relationship in the last 5 years. Change your mindset and look at the pursuit of a relationship as an opportunity that will help you grow in many ways.

Identify three issues or problems that can be converted into opportunities.

1)_____

2)_____

3)_____

Step Five

If you can dream it, you can build it: Once you've identified the issues or problems that will be converted into opportunities, start to build that idea table and begin the process by adding legs to the table. Implement specific action plans that will help turn your ideas into reality.

Idea Table No. 1: (i.e., Being in a strong relationship)
Identify Your Strengths in a Relationship
1) _____

2) _____

3) _____

Identify Your Weaknesses in a Relationship
1) _____

2) _____

3) _____

How can you convert your Weaknesses into Strengths.

1) _____

2) _____

3) _____

Step Six

Short term plans: Describe five detailed action plans that you will be pursuing over the next 30 days. What specific actions will you be taking that will help you to obtain your passion goals?

Action Plans: **Date**
Completed:

1) _____   _____

2) _____   _____

3) _____   _____

4) _____   _____

5) _____   _____

Conclusion

Thank you for taking time out of your busy schedule to read Unleashing Your Passion. I sincerely appreciate the opportunity to share my thoughts and ideas to assist you in taking your life to the next level. This book took a year to write and it was definitely a labor of love. The objective and intent of the book is to inspire you to get moving in the right direction. Breaking down and understanding the barriers that impede you from following your passion and purpose are very important. Additionally, writing specific goals and objectives along with implementing a specific strategy are all critically important.

Once you start to successfully implement the Six Steps, (Imagination, visualization, changing limiting beliefs, subtle mind shift, building the idea table and action plans) you will begin to experience subtle positive changes in your life. Your life will begin to have deeper meaning, purpose and direction.

I truly wish you the best of luck in your passion journey as this process will enrich your life. As we all move ahead with our passion journey, I welcome the opportunity to hear about your successes and challenges. The best learning will always come from the collective thoughts of individuals coming together as one. Please visit me on the web at **www.livingafulfilledlife.net** and email me as I would love to hear about and share your passion journey.

Key Points from the book

1) Keep your heart, mind and soul away from barriers and distractions that will prevent you from obtaining your passion or purpose in life.

2) Clearly visualize and imagine your passion and purpose on a daily basis.

3) Your beliefs, thoughts and action plans will become your reality so be cognizant of what you are thinking and how you are acting.

4) In order to take your life to the next level, you will need to step out of your comfort zone to create change.

5) "The issues and problems that we are faced with in life are God's way of cleverly providing us with wonderful opportunities." - Les Brown

6) Remember the importance of enhancing your *dash* in life as this truly defines your life and the contributions that you make. What is your legacy and how do you want to be remembered by peers, family and friends?

7) Don't quit your full time job just yet! Practice and fine-tune your passion while still being gainfully employed. Pursuing a passion without food, shelter and clothing will not be a pleasant endeavor.

8) Finding your passion is all about creating a life you are in love with. Create a vision of your ideal life and set goals to get you there.

9) Long term success will be defined by your ability to establish, execute and follow through with a developed plan of action on a daily basis.

10) Creating your legacy and enhancing your *dash* begins today. Make the   commitment that you will live each day with purpose and direction by asserting yourself in a way that provides inspiration and meaning to both you and the people that you come in contact with.

> *"Passion is the natural Aphrodisiac that will*
> *fuel your life with purpose and direction."*
> — *J. Drew Bycoskie*

Visit us on the web at **www.livingafulfilledlife.net**

Made in USA - North Chelmsford, MA
1312984_9781542772358
05.03.2022 1558